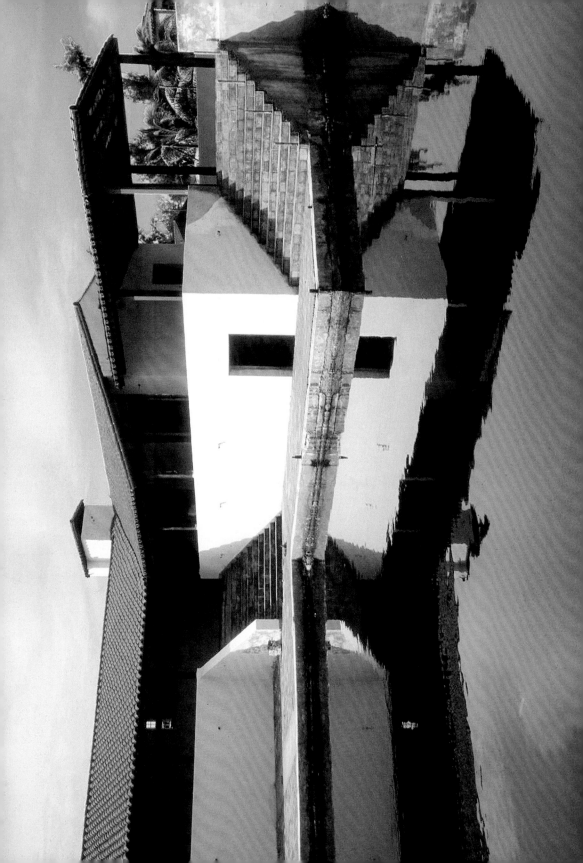

Carlos Raúl Villanueva,
Aula Magna, Universidad
Central de Venezuela,
1954.
Sculpture by Alexander Calder.

Costa, Niemeyer, et al.
Ministry of Education and Health,
Rio de Janeiro,
1937–43.

Affonso Reidy,
Museum of Modern Art,
Rio de Janeiro,
1954–65.

Oscar Niemeyer,
architect's own house at Canoa,
Rio de Janeiro,
1953.

Oscar Niemeyer,
Tancredo Neues Building,
Belo Horizonte, Brazil,
1954.

Oscar Niemeyer,
casino at Pampulha,
state of Minas Gerais, Brazil,
1942.

Carlos Raúl Villanueva,
Plaza Cubierta,
Universidad Central de Venezuela,
1954.
Sculpture by Henri Laurens.
Mural by Fernand Léger.

Carlos Raúl Villanueva,
Aula Magna,
Universidad Central
de Venezuela,
1954.
Sculpture by Alexander Calder.

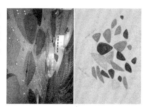

Alexander Calder,
sketch for *Clouds for Aula Magna*,
1952.

Carlos Raúl Villanueva,
lobby of Aula Magna,
Universidad Central
de Venezuela,
1954.

Eladio Dieste,
Atlántida Church,
Atlántida, Uruguay,
1958.

Gonzalo Fonseca,
Muro Blanco,
1977.
Private collection,
Caracas.

Luis Barragán,
Egerstrom Stables,
State of Mexico,
1967.

Mario Pani, Enrique del Moral,
Salvador Ortega Flores,
Administration Building,
National University,
Mexico City,
1953.

Mario Pani,
Alemán urban center,
1947–49.

Eugenio Battista,
Eutimio Falla Bonet House,
Havana,
1938.

Max Borges Recio,
Santiago Claret House,
Havana,
1941.

Max Borges Recio,
residential building,
Havana,
1938.

Eladio Dieste,
Detail of Frugoni Warehouse,
Montevideo,
1955.

Oscar Niemeyer,
Palace of the Dawn,
Brasilia,
1956–58.

LATIN AMERICAN ARCHITECTURE 1929–1960
CONTEMPORARY REFLECTIONS

Edited by
Carlos Brillembourg

The Monacelli Press

First published in the United States
of America in 2004 by
The Monacelli Press, Inc.
902 Broadway
New York, NY 10010

Printed and bound in Italy

Designed by Field Study

**Library of Congress Cataloging-in-
Publication Data**

Latin American architecture, 1929–1960 :
contemporary reflections / edited by
Carlos Brillembourg.
p. cm.
Includes bibliographical references.
ISBN 1-58093-136-7

1. Architecture—Latin America—20th century.
I. Brillembourg, Carlos.
NA702.5.L38 2004
920'.98'0904—dc22

2004000402

CONTENTS

Acknowledgments

Special gratitude is extended to Sondra Farganis, Terence Riley, and Patricia Cisneros; without their separate initiatives, the conference "Latin American Architecture: Contemporary Reflections" would not have been held and this anthology would not exist. A great debt is owed to the critics and architects who have so generously contributed to this anthology: José Antonio Aldrete-Haas, Lauro Cavalcanti, Kenneth Frampton, Jorge Francisco Liernur, and Roberto Segre, and also to Mario Gandelsonas, Monica Ponce de Leon, Enrique Norten, Paulina Villanueva, Rafael Viñoly, and Ruth Verde Zein for making the roundtable discussion such a success. Further thanks are due to Laura Beiles, Rachel Judlowe, and Peter Thiede from the Museum of Modern Art, New York; Monica Combellas and Larrisa Hernandez from the Villanueva Foundation; Sandy Rower from the Calder Foundation; Katia Mindlin; Federica Zanco from the Barragán Foundation; and Cecilia de Torres. Special thanks are due to Roy Brooks and Matthew Peterson from Field Study and to Elizabeth Kugler, Evan Schoninger, and Sasha Cutter from the Monacelli Press. Particular mention must be made of those architects who, over the years, contributed to my understanding of architecture in Latin America, among them Graziano Gasparini, Carlos Guinand Baldo, Francisca Benitez, Pilar Ortiz, Martin Vegas, Jesus Tenreiro, Enrique Fernandez-Shaw, Carlos Gomez de Llarena, Hannia Gomez, Maria Isabel Espinosa, Manuel Delgado, Pablo and Silvia Lasala, Federico Vegas, Gonzalo Fonseca, Oscar Niemeyer, Silvana Paternostro, Jimmy Alcock, and Rogelio Salmona.

CARLOS BRILLEMBOURG

Foreword

Some years ago, an Australian acquaintance was explaining to me his interpretation of some aspect of that national culture: "After all," he said, "we are a New World country." Not all of his compatriots agree with this view; some, I found, very much disagree. But I found it provocative and continue to think of the implications of his view today. The global axis of the New World, as traditionally conceived, lends itself to the polar oppositions that have served as a kind of cultural shorthand for defining the north and the south. While useful to a degree, this shorthand can also be seen as a restraint in terms of developing more sophisticated models. At worst, this shorthand lends itself to the creation of stereotypes. Indeed, the primary opposition, Anglo-Saxon versus Latin, seems to be less reliable as North America becomes more diverse in cultural heritage and, not least of all, more Latin.

In the 1950s, the Museum of Modern Art contributed to this polar construction by producing two compare-and-contrast exhibitions that showcased postwar modern architecture in the north and the south: *Built in U.S.A: Post-war Architecture* and *Latin American*

Architecture since 1945, both with catalogs written by Henry-Russell Hitchcock. Both efforts looked back at the decade of peacetime growth that had transformed modern architecture from its prewar avant-guard radicalism to a more or less accepted, if not official, style. Both cast the emergence of modern architecture in the north and south as a projection of European principles. Both were characterized by a fairly optimistic view of the modern future. Why, given that Hitchcock even referred to the latter as a "parallel or pendant" effort to the former, didn't he simply see them as a single effort? If today it is easier to imagine a single volume representing that moment, it may be due, ironically, to the essentially postmodern condition of both North and South America today, inhabited as they are by aging modern masterworks that are often as unrepeatable as they are splendid.

The inclusion of Australia among New World nations may not be historically correct, but at the outset of the twenty-first century, it can also be seen as intellectually stimulating. What happens to our concept of the New World if it is no longer dependent on a geographic axis that supports an oppositional duality but rather exists within the dynamic of a triangular array between the three continents? What would the New World mean? Each of them—North America, Latin America, and Australia—might be seen as European projects that took root in the lands of a native people. Despite Australia's largely symbolic ties to Britain, each of them has forged an independent national identity that is inseparable from the concept of modernity. Underlying their national identity, each of them today comprises multiple cultural identities, including remnants of both the colonial culture and the native culture they usurped. Each, I would maintain, is uniquely poised to contribute to the creation of contemporary culture.

TERENCE RILEY
The Philip Johnson Chief Curator
The Museum of Modern Art, New York

One finds in this world a great deal of injustice
but there is one about which no one ever speaks—
the injustice of the climate.

ALBERT CAMUS

Introduction

The conference "Latin American Architecture 1929–1960, Contemporary Reflections" was held on October 11, 2002, at the New School University in New York. It was sponsored jointly by the Vera List Center of The New School University and the Architecture Department of the Museum of Modern Art, New York. This conference originated in the search for critical tools that would allow us to understand and reflect upon the specific architectural contributions of Latin American architecture during the period framed by the great crisis of 1929 and the end of the second postwar era. The European conflict that began in 1939 opened a new phase of economic and social opportunities for Latin America, spurred by a rise in the price of raw materials and food products, which coincided with social struggles as people sought popular participation in the local governments. The essays in this anthology will outline the complex exchange of ideas coming and going between Europe, North America, and Latin America at this time.

Architecture produced fifty years ago in Latin America was central to the international development of modern architecture. Parallel to this axiom is the idea that this architecture has been forgotten or misunderstood in mainstream histories. The concept of a "Latin American architecture" is denied, and what has prevailed is a regional understanding based on each country's architectural masters and a somewhat limited understanding of the rich cultural interchange that produced such extraordinary work. Absorbing the teachings of Le Corbusier, this architecture eradicated the boundary between interior and exterior in the benevolence of a warm climate. In Latin America, Northern European architecture became a colored and continuous sequence of interior and exterior spaces open to the landscape. Technical and formal innovations abounded in reinforced-concrete structures: the thin-shell structures of Felix Candela, the weightless columns of Niemeyer's Palace of the Dawn, the complex concrete-and-steel structure of Affonso Reidy's Museum of Modern Art in Rio, the chiaroscuro light filtered by a concrete lattice in Villanueva's covered plaza, and the undulating brick-and-steel structures of Eladio Dieste's Atlántida Church are but a few examples of a new vocabulary that combines a tectonic attitude toward structure with a fluid conception of space and landscape. This autonomous architecture without doctrinaire qualities is free to explore and expand upon the legacy of a more hermetic European modernism.

A complex ensemble of territories and traditions comprises Latin America, forming a unity made evident in its urban culture. The three-hundred-year colonial era produced architectural and urban innovations in the new and ancient cities: Lima, Cuzco, Mexico City, Quito, Antigua, Cartagena, Santo Domingo, Havana, Bogotá, Caracas, Buenos Aires, and Rio de Janeiro. The symbiosis of the Spanish and Portuguese settlers with the ancient agrarian or nomad cultures such as the Incas, Mayans, Caribs, or Aztecs; a newly evangelized Amerindian population; and a captive African one produced an original culture whose identity fluctuates among and through its inhabitants.

Colonial mannerist and baroque architecture, from an eclectic mix of Flemish, German, French, Italian, and Spanish influences, was built by priest-architects using as manuals the latest European engravings and treatises, which provided a solid foundation for the art of building cities. It was this combination of scholarship, craftsmanship, and isolation that allowed for the creative essence of colonial American architecture. In the early nineteenth century, a war of independence begun by Simon Bolívar, José de San Martin, and Don Bernardo O'Higgins, following the example set by George Washington, disrupted the foundations of these colonial societies; after a long and bloody struggle, independent republics were established that were politically and economically unstable. A period of civil wars ensued. During this time, a consensus arose in these new republics against the Spanish colonial legacy, and the ideology of scientific, technological, and economic progress started to take hold. The public realm was modernized by adapting neoclassical French urban and architectural models. Thus boulevards with freestanding Beaux-Arts-style institutional buildings appeared within the colonial grid.

From 1929 to 1960 cultural and architectural innovations followed the political renovation by both democratic and authoritarian governments in Argentina, Uruguay, Brazil, Venezuela, Mexico, Cuba, and Santo Domingo. Although the circumstances of this cultural transformation are particular to each country, the State's role in promoting excellence in public architecture was the norm. This transformation took place at a time when the cultural and economic production in Europe and the United States was diminished by the war. The patronage by progressive and sometimes authoritative States allowed for the significant contribution of these heretofore peripheral countries to the universal language of architecture. This was not a "critical regionalism" but, during those thirty-one years, this architecture became central to the development of modern architecture, as the previous centers (Berlin, Paris, London, and New York) were exhausted by World War II.

Each essay in this volume examines a particular architecture within a specific region. The conventional history of this period highlights the eight so-called Latin American masters: Eladio Dieste, Oscar Niemeyer, Joaquín Torres Garcia, Lucio Costa, Amancio Williams, Juan O'Gorman, Luis Barragán, and Carlos Raúl Villanueva. In this anthology, that historical cliché is put aside in favor of a closer inspection of the wide-ranging cultural forces at work in the creation of what we will call the "golden age" of Latin American architecture. The book is not meant as a comprehensive survey of this period, and it does not include excellent work done in Chile, Ecuador, Colombia, Panama, Costa Rica, Guatemala, Honduras, and Nicaragua during this period. It is my opinion that the future of architectural production depends upon a better understanding of the cultural renovation evident in this work. One could argue that the thin shells of Felix Candela in Mexico inspired architects not only in Venezuela and Cuba but also architects like Eero Saarinen, who produced the TWA terminal at JFK airport; a contemporary mannered version in bent steel trusses covered in metal shingles would be Frank Gehry's museum in Bilbao.

In September 1929, when Le Corbusier was invited to lecture in Buenos Aires, Montevideo, and Rio de Janeiro, he was received by a culture ready to apply and transform European modernism to the pressing needs of a new and vibrant economy. In 1925 the Russian-born Brazilian architect Gregori Warchavchik, of São Paolo, published his *Manifesto of Functional Architecture*. His text made use of the term *functional architecture* before the publication of Alberto

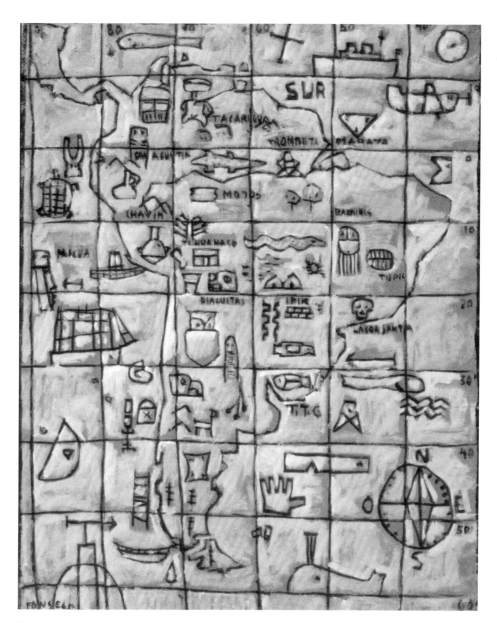

Gonzalo Fonseca,
map of South America,
1950.
Private collection,
Montevideo.

Le Corbusier,
Urban Studies Projects for Montevideo,
Uruguay, and São Paulo, Brazil.
Aerial perspectives:
Montevideo, above; São Paulo, below.
1929.
Emilio Ambasz Fund, 1985.Collection of the Museum of Modern Art, New York.

Sartoris's *Elements of Functional Architecture* (1932). Le Corbusier presented an expansion plan for Rio in the form of a coastal highway with housing underneath; it was partly inspired by the flights he took with the pilot Antoine de Saint-Exupéry. By the time Le Corbusier returned to Brazil in 1936 to work with Lucio Costa and his team of young architects (Oscar Niemeyer, Affonso Reidy, and Jorge Moreira) on the University City and the Ministry of Education, modern architecture had already taken hold throughout Brazil, Argentina, and Uruguay. At this time the most progressive school of architecture on the American continent, based on the teachings of the Bauhaus, was the School of Architecture and Engineering in Montevideo under the leadership of Julio Vilamajó.

The New York World's Fair of 1939–40 began a golden period for America's modern architecture. The Brazilian pavilion, designed by Lucio Costa and Oscar Niemeyer with interiors by Paul Lester Wiener, was the most innovative pavilion with its ramped entry, *brise-soleil*, and a curved perimeter curtain wall dissolving the edge between interior and exterior. After seeing the pavilion, Mayor La Guardia awarded Oscar Niemeyer the keys to the city of New York. The firm Skidmore, Owings & Merrill, with a young Gordon Bunshaft in charge, designed the Venezuelan pavilion, a modern glass box with a long, inclined exterior roof reminiscent of the Russian pavilion in the Paris world exhibition of 1937.

In the early 1960s a kind of Pan-American modernism took hold, due to the enormous influence of Oscar Niemeyer's work in Brasilia (1956–60) and the United Nations (1947). Architects such as Wallace Harrison, Max Abramovitz, and Philip Johnson produced work indebted to Niemeyer in projects such as Lincoln Center (1962–66), the Museum of Modern Art's sculpture garden (1953), Water Pavilion at the Glass House (1949), and the Albany Mall (1962–78).

Political agendas of the time reflected the architect's fundamental role in transforming society. With the construction of Brasilia (1956–60), the government of Juscelino Kubitschek in Brazil set in motion the ideal collaboration between two architects and society as a whole. Inaugurating the new capital, Kubitschek said, "More than a mere aesthetic trend, and above all more than the projection into our culture of a universal movement, [it is] a solution that takes carefully into account climate and scenery, perhaps the most original and precise expression of the creative intelligence of modern Brazil." Here the marriage of socialism and modern architecture was put to the test. With the construction of Palace of the Dawn, Brasilia's first building, Niemeyer synthesized the poured-concrete plastic forms of his early work with the concept of "universal space" coming from the work of Mies van der Rohe. The result is a new type of monumentality in a landscape that appears infinite. Within this horizontal axis, the monumental government buildings, symbolic of a new country, appear as modest interruptions in a powerful, almost extraterrestrial landscape.

Is the architecture of Brasilia a "humanistic afterimage embedded within our collective memory as the substance of an idyllic dream," as Kenneth Frampton writes in his preface to *Latin American Architecture: Six Voices*? Brasilia, which was designed for a maximum of 700,000 inhabitants, has more than 1.5 million inhabitants today and seems to be growing rapidly by the incorporation of satellite cities on its periphery. The dream of a pansocial city proved to be idyllic. This city, designed for enlightened and privileged civil servants traveling by automobiles through a city without traffic lights, has become a complex modern city with suburbs for the rich and the poor.

The loss of social purpose in architectural projects has disrupted the integral conception of art and architecture within a given culture. Is it not inevitable that architecture must anticipate social ideals? When architecture becomes mimetic of the status quo, it becomes reactionary and academic. The critical power of this golden period resides in an architecture that speaks about the necessary social pact of the architect with society as a whole. And yet the utopian dreams of changing society through architecture were frustrated in each case. Visions of towers in a landscaped urban park became the nightmare of suburban sprawl and urban renewal. The contemporary crisis manifests itself, on the one hand, as a globalized architecture dedicated to commodity fetishism, and on the other, as the explosion of a new slum urbanism surrounding most Third World cities, threatening the public nature of the city and making architecture somewhat irrelevant.

Let us keep in mind that Le Corbusier was not the only foreigner to set his sights on Latin America at this time. Mexico became a haven for surrealism with the arrival of Luis Buñuel, André Breton, Max Ernst, Leonora Carrington, Tina Modotti, and Edward Weston. Venezuela was a haven for modern art and architecture with the building of the University City by Carlos Raúl Villanueva, and the projects by Gio Ponti, Oscar Niemeyer, Roberto Burle-Marx, Wallace Harrison, Richard Neutra, Paul Lester Wiener, José Lluis Sert, and Marcel Breuer. Elsewhere we find important works by Alberto Sartoris, Mario Piacentini, Town Planning Associates, Edward Durrell Stone, and Max Abramovitz. Yet it was in Brazil that this renewed modernity produced the most prolific and influential architecture. In 1928 the poet Oswald de Andrade published his *Manifesto Anthropófago*, which advocates a "metaphorical cannibalism" as a defense against cultural colonialism. His manifesto argues that the identity of Brazilian culture is the result of a transformation of imported European culture by a process of "cultural cannibalism." By the 1950s Brazilian architectural culture had matured to the extent that it began to be exported. Roberto Burle-Marx was commissioned to design and build his largest urban park in Caracas, and Oscar Niemeyer went on to design and build, over the next seventy years, projects in Caracas, New York, Israel, Paris, Milan, Algiers, and London.

The sponsorship of a progressive modern architecture by both democratic and authoritarian regimes from 1929 to 1960 underlined the common desire to build a progressive twentieth-century industrialized society. For the most part, this project was left incomplete. It is not our task in this book to analyze the reasons for its demise but rather to understand the extraordinary architecture that was produced and still stands, emboding the very essence, or *rasa* of a universal architecture. It is evident that Latin America is no longer the same continent that it was in 1929, when Le Corbusier foresaw the future of modern architecture. In the following essays and in the roundtable discussion that concludes this volume, we will discuss the most innovative work of this period done in Brazil, Argentina, Uruguay, Venezuela, Mexico, and Cuba with the hope of reversing a long period of deliberate historical amnesia.

CARLOS BRILLEMBOURG

LE CORBUSIER AND OSCAR NIEMEYER: INFLUENCE AND COUNTER-INFLUENCE, 1929–1965

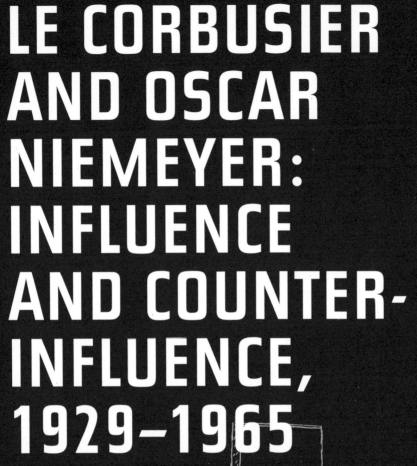
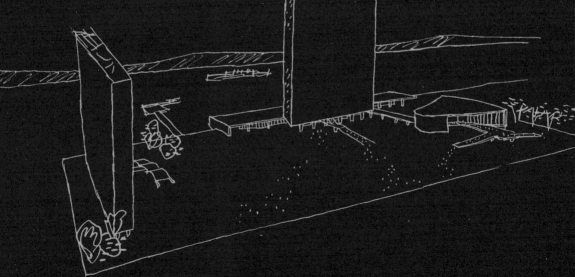

KENNETH
FRAMPTON

And I am sure that your emotion will be intense and reassuring when you see face to face for the first time, the ministry building and when you pass your hand over its magnificent pilotis rising to ten meters in height. And it will be equally comforting for you to confirm on the spot that the generous seed disseminated over the four corners of the earth from Buenos Aires to Stockholm, from New York to Moscow and widely spread in this dear Brazilian earth—thanks to the exceptional but unsuspected talent of Oscar and his group—is now blossoming into a flowering architecture, the grace and charm of which is already beneficial to us.

LUCIO COSTA, JUNE 18, 1946[1]

Oscar Niemeyer,
Scheme 32,
United Nations,
New York,
1947.
Perspective.

Le Corbusier's first experience of Latin America, which lasted from late September to early December 1929, was something of an epiphany, as is suggested by the sketches that he made during his sojourn. His airplane trips over the continent, in the company of the pioneer aviator Jean Mermoz, inspired him to imagine vast urban extensions, integrated into the landscape at an unprecedented scale. São Paulo and Montevideo were successively rendered as viaduct cities, while his expansion scheme for Rio de Janeiro consisted of a coastal megastructure, elevated above the ground and carrying beneath its roadbed some fifteen residential floors. Rio's panoramic corniche seems to have heightened that "oceanic" aspect of his vision, embodying a peculiarly mystical sense of union with the universe.[2]

As Jean-Pierre Giordani has remarked, Le Corbusier's time in Brazil was probably the happiest of his life, for here he felt, for the first time perhaps, that his vision of modernity could be realized on a grand scale and in a manner that was in keeping with the climate, landscape, and life of the people.[3] This affinity was confirmed by the wide following that he gained throughout the continent, particularly in Brazil, where such architects as Lucio Costa, Oscar Niemeyer, Affonso Reidy, and Jorge Moreira pursued a neo-Corbusian practice, while Marcelo and Milton Roberto were among the first to use vertical *brises-soleil* in their ABI Press Association building of 1936.

Born in 1907 in Rio de Janeiro, Oscar Niemeyer Soares Filho had yet to enter the Escola Nacional de Belas Artes when Le Corbusier first lectured in Brazil in 1929. When Le Corbusier came to Brazil for a second time in 1936 to work on the design of the Ministry of Education, Niemeyer had already graduated and was working as an assistant in the office of Lucio Costa and Carlos Leão. Le Corbusier was to be involved in the design of two major works in Rio de Janeiro during his second visit: the University City and the Ministry of Education. In addition to Costa and Carlos Leão, his collaborators during this second visit included a number of young Brazilian architects, among them Oscar Niemeyer, Affonso Reidy, Jorge Moreira, Ernani Vasconcelos, and the engineer Emilio Baumgart. Publishing the completed Ministry of Education, as realized in 1943, in his *Oeuvre Complète 1938–46*, Le Corbusier claimed credit for inventing the *brise-soleil*, as this had been initially devised for a twelve-story tower that he had projected for a cliff site in Algiers in 1933. Le Corbusier's preferred design for the Ministry of Education was an eight-story horizontal slab, of which, strangely enough, he only depicted the southern aspect, that is to say, the elevation without *brise-soleil*, facing out over the bay toward the Sugar Loaf on a site close to the airport. One is struck by the way the Brazilian team immediately refined the sun-breaker concept by introducing a system of manually adjustable louvers, capable of maintaining solar protection irrespective of the sun angle. The Costa team added other refinements to the penultimate Le Corbusier sketch for the Ministry, including raising the height of the pilotis and ornamenting the interior of the building with murals and decorative ceramic wall treatments by Candido Portinari.

Le Corbusier's Cité Universitaire project for Rio, of 1938, was more organic in its composition than the proposal he had made for a Cité Mondiale on a site close to Geneva ten years before. His obsessive use of golden section in the Cité Mondiale seems to have been abandoned, under the influence of the Costa team, in favor of a freer, more asymmetrical composition infiltrated by vegetation and by the irregular topography of the site. Something of Niemeyer's heroic dynamism is perhaps already evident in the streamlined composition of the five outriding slab blocks. Not only was the *aula magna* in this project modeled on Le Corbusier's Palais des Soviets proposal of 1931 but it was also the first occasion on which Le Corbusier's spiraling *musée à croissance illimitée* would make its appearance, as a horizontal version of his pyramidal museum initially projected as the centerpiece of the Cité Mondiale. In his book *Des canons, des munitions? Merci!... Des logis s'il vous plaît*, of 1938, Le Corbusier is at pains to point out that his Brazilian collaborators wanted to evolve a radical alternative to the campus format of the North American university.

It was a fundamental shift in Le Corbusier's own aesthetic, however, that would eventually exercise a decisive influence on Niemeyer, particularly in turning the latter's domestic work toward an intrinsically regional expression. Ironically enough, the origins of this "vernacular" seem to have had their roots in Argentina, rather than Brazil. This much is suggested by a sketch that appears in Le Corbusier's *Précisions sur un état présent de l'architecture et de l'urbanisme*, of 1930, wherein he describes a complex of agricultural buildings that he encountered during his stay in Argentina:

You say to me, "We have nothing." I answer, "You have this, a standard, and a play of forms in the Argentine light, a play of very beautiful and pure forms."... The other day, at twilight, we took a long walk in the streets of La Plata with Gonzales Garramo. Property walls like this one, for instance. Just realize the architectural fact of this little door set into the wall. The other architectural fact of the door cutting the wall in two. The third architectural fact of the big garage door. The fourth architectural fact of this narrow passage between the two properties.... The fifth architectural fact of the oblique line of the roof and its overhang![4]

It is just these tropes that would inform his remarkable Errazuris House, projected in 1930 for a site on the coast of Chile.

This house is [to be] built on the edge of the Pacific Ocean. Since one cannot command in this place craftsmanship of sufficient quality, one uses the raw materials of the place and carries out a simple work; walls made of large stone blocks, timber framing made from tree trunks, and as a result, a pitched roof. The rusticity of the materials is not in any way an obstruction to the expression of a clear plan and a modern aesthetic.[5]

The unbuilt Errazuris House is the first work in which Le Corbusier made a total break with the Purist machine aesthetic in that the double-height volume of the house was to be covered by monopitched roofs sloping inward toward a central gutter. As the above description suggests, this roof was to have been finished in terra-cotta tiles, while the rubble stone walls of the interior were to have been left unplastered. The abstract, rhythmic quality of the mass-form is deftly heightened by the discrete placement of rectangular openings—a rhythmic play that Le Corbusier had witnessed in Buenos Aires and La Plata. This rustic syntax included rough flagstone floors throughout the ground floor. Otherwise the "modernity" to which he referred depended largely on the use of narrow pedestrian ramps rising from the living room to the timber-framed sleeping level on the first floor, together with a totally glazed northern elevation and picture windows facing west over the ocean. In his *Oeuvre Complète 1929–34*, Le Corbusier remarks on the fact that this new paradigm was emulated by Antonin Raymond in his remarkable Karuizawa House, published in *Architectural Record* in 1934. Raymond's thatched-roof transposition of Le Corbusier's initial departure anticipated by five years a similar elaboration of virtually the same basic *parti* by Oscar Niemeyer, who would repatriate Le Corbusier's appropriation of the Latin American vernacular to its roots.

We encounter this for the first time in 1939 in the Passos House that Niemeyer projected for a remote mountainous site at Miguel Pereira, three hours from Rio de Janeiro by train. As Niemeyer's description indicates, this was largely conceived as an "open-air" weekend house where the small dining/living space with its diminutive kitchen opens onto a continuous L-shaped veranda. As Stamo Papadaki describes it: "The living room is only a small sheltered part of the total living area. The three bedrooms which occupy the second floor have individual sleeping porches. The continuous low-pitched roof shelters the two-story and the one-story parts of the house."[6] One notes that the end walls of the Passos House are of unplastered rubble stonework, much like the weekend house that Le Corbusier realized at Mathes, near Lyons, in 1935. The timber framing and balustrading of the Passos House seem to derive from this source rather than from the Errazuris project.

This neo-vernacular reference did not show itself in the *parti* for the Brazilian pavilion erected for the New York World's Fair of 1939. While still vaguely Corbusian in character, this work, designed by Niemeyer, in association with Lucia Costa and Paul Lester Wiener, departed radically from the Purist syntax by introducing a formal undulation that anticipated the plasticity of Niemeyer's subsequent production. This organicism is also evident in the sweep of the wide pedestrian entry ramp that swings into the bent, L-shaped mass of the building in such a way as to cut open the roof of the first-floor portico while playing off the hyperbolic plan-form of the adjacent auditorium. This extravagant gesture ricochets throughout the ground floor of the pavilion as the various set pieces—orchid house, bird house, and aquarium—bend and weave through the steel *pilotis* that sustain the upper floor of the building. Hence the botanical/zoological exhibits combine in a syncopated microlandscape with a coffee bar, a restaurant, and a circular dance floor. The intention was to display Brazil as a tropical country of unparalleled exoticism.

The neo-vernacular adopted for the hotel that Niemeyer built the following year at Ouro Preto, in the state of Minas Gerais, was only too appropriate in that the structure was erected in the midst of an

Brazilian pavilion,
New York World's Fair,
1939.

Le Corbusier,
Second scheme for the
Ministry of Education
and Health, 1939.

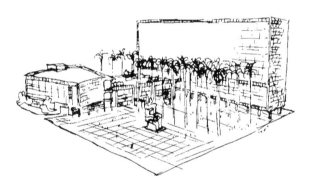

Oscar Niemeyer,
architect's own house,
Rio de Janeiro,
1942.

eighteenth-century Baroque colonial city that had just been declared a national monument and was thus under the protection of the Servicio do Patrimonio Historico e Artistico Nacional. Of this self-conscious insertion of a new structure into an old fabric Niemeyer wrote:

The placing of the building on stilts results in an unobstructed view from the pedestrian level; the general bulk of the building is reduced by limiting the number of the bedroom floors to two. The tiles of the sloping roof, the occasional use of stone from the nearby Itacomi Mountain and the adoption of the same colors which are predominant in the town contribute to an organic blending of this building with its historical setting while avoiding narrow applications of dead styles. The lobby and the principal social rooms are located on the second floor, accessible through a ramp. On one side of the third floor corridor there is a row of small guest rooms with shower baths, and, on the other side of the same corridor, the living rooms of duplex units. The latter extend to an open terrace and are connected with spiral stairs to a bedroom and bath on the fourth floor. There is no corridor on the fourth floor.[7]

Through its sectional organization, this hotel already reveals the relaxed way in which Niemeyer would reinterpret the Purist legacy of Le Corbusier, whose Pavillon de l'Esprit Nouveau of 1925 was the origin for the duplex units occupying the upper floors of the hotel.

In 1942 Niemeyer built a house for himself in the Gavea section of Rio de Janeiro. This was, in effect, a two-story neo-vernacular dwelling raised on concrete *pilotis* facing out over a lake. Here, as in Le Corbusier's Errazuris project, a ramp extends over half the length of the building and serves to connect the four levels of the house: the archi-tect's studio, the living/dining space, a mezzanine, and two bedrooms at the highest level. The sculptural mass-form and the cantilevered living-room terrace facing out over the lake are both subtly offset by sliding horizontal shutters, painted dark blue, and a monopitched roof finished with red tiles. Niemeyer had first attempted this hybrid synthesis in the equally neo-vernacular Cavalcanti House of 1940.

In 1942 Niemeyer was at work on another house in much the same vein, designed for Herbert Johnson, proprietor of the Johnson Wax Company of Racine, Wisconsin. By this date Frank Lloyd Wright had already built two remarkable works for Johnson in Racine; the S.C. Johnson and Son Administration Building and Johnson's own residence, Wingspread, both of 1937. Johnson's presence in Brazil was due to the fact that he imported wax from the Brazilian state of Ceará. Hence he commissioned a house there for himself and his agent. This luxurious vacation dwelling at Fortaleza was designed to take advantage of the cooling breezes coming off a nearby lake. It comprised a three-story house with services at grade and the main living on the first floor, with sleeping accommodations above. This last was treated as a mezzanine overlooking a central double-height space. Structured about a reinforced-concrete frame, this building, much like the Passos House, encompassed a two-story-high patio overlooking the lake.

Of greater consequence for Niemeyer's emergence as the leading Brazilian architect were the remarkable civic works that he projected in collaboration with the engineer Emilio Baumgart in the early 1940s; a water tower-cum-belvedere for Ribeirao das Lages, and a competition entry for the National Athletic Center in Rio de Janeiro, once again organized under patronage of the Minister of Education, Gustavo Capanema. The program comprised an Olympic swimming pool and seating for 10,000 people; three covered stadia (one each for gymnastics, basketball, and tennis) with a 5,000-person seating capacity; and a large stadium for 130,000 spectators. In addition, there was a polo field, a school for physical education, and a football pitch.

In many respects Niemeyer's stadium is a synthesis of two of Le Corbusier's most remarkable monumental projects: his entry for the Palais des Soviets competition of 1931, and the stadium of his Centre National de Réjouissances Populaires, capable of accommodating an assembly of 100,000 people. Le Corbusier approached the challenge of sheltering such a large span of seating from rain and sun with two different structural propositions: on the one hand, a single mast that anchored the cables of a velarium covering the seating, on the other, a semi-rigid roof suspended over the seating and supported by a catenary cable structure.

Le Corbusier's turn toward tensile construction came with the exposed, radial beams of the large hall in his Palais des Soviets submission, wherein a hyperbolic reinforced-concrete arch picked up the ends of the radial beams through cables suspended from the arch. As in the alternative stadium roof structure proposed by Le Corbusier, Niemeyer would opt for a cable-suspended semi-rigid roof over his stadium seating, with the cables hanging from a three-hundred-meter-span hyperbolic arch. There are other similarities between the two stadia, above all, the fact that they were both partially recessed into the ground. Of this hybrid solution Niemeyer wrote:

If the stadium were to be built on the ground level it would be necessary to develop ramps long enough to reach a thirteen-story building: but it is obvious that such a solution would result in an extremely cumbersome structure.... A design was adopted which calls for a stadium level 42 feet below the ground. This solution makes possible a lower structure with shorter ramps.[8]

Like Le Corbusier, Niemeyer envisaged his stadium being used for other kinds of mass spectacles besides sports, including "civic ceremonies, pageants and military parades." The asymmetrical character

Oscar Niemeyer and
Emilio Baumgart, engineer,
National Athletic Center,
Rio de Janeiro,
1941.
Aerial view of model.

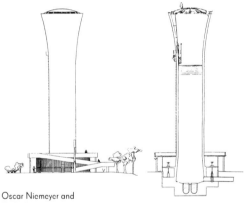

Oscar Niemeyer and
Emilio Baumgart, engineer,
water tower,
Ribeirao dos Lages, Brazil,
1934.
Elevation and section.

Oscar Niemeyer,
casino,
Pampulha,
1942.
Foyer with access ramps.

of both arenas testifies to this, as do their prominent rostrums and wide vomitories that allow for military parades to pass through the stadium. The Corbusian influence also extends to the monumental role played by the hyperbolic arch itself which, as in Le Corbusier's Palais des Soviets proposal, is intended to serve as a civic symbol from a great distance, much like the spires and domes of Christendom in a medieval city.

Baumgart evidently played a fundamental role in the development of this project, as he did in the design of the water tower. This last was projected as a flared concrete cylinder, rising out of an elevated platform-cum-belvedere. The square platform, covering the pump room at grade, was patently influenced by the ground floor of Le Corbusier's Villa Savoye, while the sweeping monumental ramp accessing this roof clearly recalls the ramp of Niemeyer's 1939 Brazilian pavilion. One has the feeling that the great Brazilian tradition of heroic reinforced-concrete construction has much of its origins in this fertile collaboration.[9]

In many respects the casino at Pampulha, realized in 1942, near Belo Horizonte, is the ultimate neo-Corbusian building of Niemeyer's early career. Of reinforced-concrete construction throughout and designed with the engineer Joaquim Cardozo, it is, once again, a transposition of Corbusier's Villa Savoye of 1929. Apart from fundamental differences in terms of size and program, the most dramatic shift resides in the structure itself: for a while the freestanding column grid of Pampulha is predicated on a four-by-five-bay square grid, that of the Villa Savoye is a four-by-four-bay system with cantilevered extensions front and back. Since the narrower cantilever in Niemeyer's case is the same on all four sides, he is able to articulate the columns within the prism with greater clarity than in the Villa Savoye. The other fundamental departure at the level of the *parti* is the role played by the ramp: in Le Corbusier's design it runs up the central axis of the building in a narrow slot which, for all its spatial ingenuity, reveals its full plastic potential only at the roof terrace, where the dynamism of its figurative form becomes visible as the ramp culminates in the solarium on the roof. The ramp in Niemeyer's casino plays a totally different role since it stands free in the midst of a generous foyer as it rises up, first, to provide access to a theater/nightclub at the rear of the building and, second, to give access to the game room on the first floor. This last is L-shaped in plan and overlooks the ramp as it ascends amid the freestanding columns of the foyer.

Where the Villa Savoye stands aloof in the landscape, Niemeyer's casino is not only symptomatic of his emerging organic manner but also profoundly responsive to the promontory on which it sits, above a lake. Thus the lounge that flows out of the foyer under the game room leads to a cafe terrace with steps descending to the water's edge. Another auxiliary stair issues from the soffit of the nightclub. The lakeside terrace is served by a bar at the head of a service spine under the casino. This element, containing dressing rooms, is linked by a spiral stair to the backstage of the nightclub above.

The lyrical ingenuity of the various itineraries that attend this plan is of an exceptional precision. We are witness to a moment in which the Corbusian free plan extends into the exotic topography of the Brazilian landscape. At the same time, Niemeyer's use of vertical industrial glazing, reminiscent of the Villa Savoye, maintains a crystalline severity against the plasticity of the concrete. The finishing touch of a concrete canopy, cantilevering off steel tubes, together with a reclining figure, imparts a playfully honorific character to the front of the building. Thus the overall aura is alternately both severe and exotic, particularly with respect to the interior, where the cylindrical columns are clad with chromium steel and the concrete upstands are faced in Argentine onyx. Elsewhere pink-tinted mirror revetment is offset by tufted satin wall linings while the glass dance floor is lit from beneath. Such exoticism, bordering on decadence, removes us totally from the polychromatic, painterly character of the Purist ethos.

With Niemeyer's Casa do Baile, Dancehall and Restaurant (1942), situated on the edge of the same artificial lake, the cylindrical columns of the free plan become totally liberated as they follow the undulating form of a flat cantilevered canopy that meanders out from the circular drum of the restaurant to culminate in a small circular stage. This obsession with circular form also governs the perimeter of the service bustle to the rear of the restaurant. As everywhere else in Niemeyer's Pampulha complex, there is a dance floor in the center of the restaurant.

The implicit hedonism of Niemeyer's manner is fully consummated here by the gardens of Henrique Lahmeyer de Mello Barreto and Roberto Burle Marx, the latter having already been responsible for the gardens of the Ministry of Education. Niemeyer's quintessential exotic palette of the 1940s is completed at this juncture by blue and white Portuguese azaleas that are particularly evident in Pampulha, in the yacht club and the Saint Francis of Assisi church. Together with a rustic weekend house designed for the then mayor of Belo Horizonte, Juscelino Kubitcheck, these structures, enriched by Portinari, complete the Pampulha sequence erected around the shores of an artificial lake. In this complex, aided by the vision of Burle Marx, Niemeyer freed himself from the ethos of Purism. Nowhere is this more explicit than in a resort hotel projected for Pampulha in 1943, where the public rooms on the ground floor flow out into a lakeside garden, to become virtually inseparable from the exotic vegetation and landscape. A similar *mariage de contours* informs a seafront vacation house projected for the Tremaine family in Santa Barbara, California, some four years earlier.

Oscar Niemeyer, Lucio Costa, and Paul Lester Wiener,
Brazilian pavilion,
New York World's Fair,
1939.

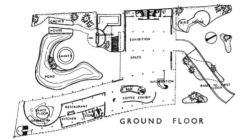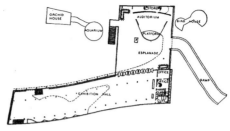

Brazilian pavilion,
New York World's Fair,
1939.

Oscar Niemeyer,
Casa do Baile Dancehall
and Restaurant,
Pampulha, Minas Gerais, Brazil,
1940.

Oscar Niemeyer,
yacht club,
Pampulha, Minas Gerais, Brazil,
1940.
Sketch.

Oscar Niemeyer,
resort hotel,
Pampulha, Minas Gerais, Brazil,
1940.
Perspective.

Oscar Niemeyer,
Modern Art Museum,
Caracas, Venezuela, 1955.
Project.

Something of Le Corbusier's rationalism is still evident at an urbanistic scale, however, in Niemeyer's projects of the mid-1940s: above all, the plan for an aeronautical training center at São José dos Campos of 1947 and the so-called Scheme 32 for the United Nations Headquarters in New York, dating from the same year. It may be more correct, however, to see this period as one of a mutually enriching exchange between master and pupil. It is difficult to ignore the contrast between the freely undulating circulation and the rational layout of the slab blocks in Niemeyer's aeronautical school and how this contrast is echoed in Le Corbusier's plan for the extension of La Rochelle–La Pallice, of April 1946. At this juncture, it is difficult to know who was influencing whom; the same can be said for their respective proposals in 1947 for the United Nations, New York, with Niemeyer's project 32 and Le Corbusier's project 23A amounting to virtually the same *parti*.[10]

Niemeyer's increasing independence manifested itself in two otherwise rather sober urban blocks designed by him in the second half of the 1940s; the Boavista Bank, realized in Rio de Janeiro in 1946, and the printing works, Emprezas Gráficas, of 1949. Both of these multistory structures deploy an orthogonal freestanding column grid plus *brise-soleil* on all facades except the south. The Boavista building stands out in Niemeyer's early period for the remarkably fluid and luminous character of the banking hall, with an undulating, double-height glass-block wall and a sweeping, travertine counter. The Emprezas Gráficas is equally compelling for the ingenious manner in which the column grid runs through all floors so as to be equally convenient in its bay spacing for the accommodation of offices on its upper floors and for the position of off-loading bays for trucks at the second floor.

The brilliant flexibility of Niemeyer's planning during this period seems to surface fifteen years later in Le Corbusier's proposal for a congress hall in Strasbourg (1963–64), which, with its exposed ramps sweeping out of the building and its dynamic organic internal planning, is surely the most Brazilian work of his entire career. The same may also be said for his project for the Olivetti cybernetic center in Rho-Milan of virtually the same date: the organicism of its form and of the site layout seems to derive its biological character in part from the internal circulation and in part from the dynamic movement of a nearby high-speed autoroute. The mutual discourse between master and pupil seems to have come full circle at this juncture. The emotional bond between them remained exceptionally close throughout their association, as is testified to in Le Corbusier's *Oeuvre Complète 1957–65*, wherein, only too prophetically, we find the text of Le Corbusier's last leave-taking from Rio de Janeiro, addressed to his Brazilian friends on December 29, 1962, together with Niemeyer's response, dated January 22, 1963, which reads:

I open the books of Girsberger, Zurich—how much we can learn from them and again I see his old projects pausing at the Palace of the Soviets—one of his masterpieces—with the beautiful arch which supports the roof of the great auditorium, a solution which has been taken up by others and adapted in all sorts of ways—also by myself in the project for the National Stadium in Rio de Janeiro. I then leaf through his more recent books edited by Jean Petit and again I am moved by the feeling that he still is young in spite of his 75 years, young enough to project Ronchamp and Chandigarh in the same carefree manner he had twenty years ago! I remember our last meeting which took place in Paris in 1962. I remember above all, having been surprised to find in him the same élan, the same energy which has characterized his life, always ready to take up his old fights again if needs be, like the lone warrior who, already victorious, remains erect and alone on the field of battle, refreshed and ready for new combat.[11]

This mutual admiration is closed with Le Corbusier's death in August 1965, ten years after Niemeyer entered upon a brand of dynamic minimalism that would separate his subsequent work from the intimate lyricism of his initial maturity. As Francisco Bullrich pointed out in his 1969 survey of Latin American architecture, something bordering on science fiction begins to appear in Niemeyer's architecture in the mid-1950s, most decisively perhaps in the inverted pyramidal museum that he projects for Caracas, Venezuela, which appears as a self-conscious inversion of Le Corbusier's Musée Mondial of 1928. At the same time as Bullrich remarks:

It is difficult to see its almost incredible fantastic image as anything more than a model. The more we think about it, the more it seems completely devoid of a true purposeful possibility. In Niemeyer's models there is always something very tempting, new, forcefully expressed, and buoyant. This brings us to the somewhat critical conclusion that his buildings are very often blown-up, full-scale models.[12]

Are we not close here to the first hints of a spectacular postmodernity which now seems somewhat divorced from those subtle, programmatic articulations with which the modern movement was once inextricably associated?

Notes

1. Le Corbusier, *Oeuvre Complète, 1938–46,* ed. Willy Boesiger (Erlenbach-Zurich: Les Editions d'Architecture), 90.

2. See Sigmund Freud, *Civilization and Its Discontents* (1930) trans. James Strachey (New York: W. W. Norton, 1961–62), 11, 12. Freud uses the term *oceanic* to refer to a mystical sense of oneness with the universe, suggested to him as a primary source of spirituality by the writer Romain Rolland.

3. Jean-Pierre Giordani, in *Le Corbusier: une encyclopédie,* edited by Jacques Lucan (Paris, 1987), 402.

4. Le Corbusier, *Précisions sur un état présent de l'architecture et de l'urbanisme* (Paris: Vincent Freal, 1929), 228.

5. Le Corbusier, *Oeuvre Complète 1938–46* (Zurich: Les Editions Girsberger), 48.

6. Stamo Papadaki, *The Work of Oscar Niemeyer* (New York: Reinhold, 1948), 20.

7. Niemeyer, quoted in *The Work of Oscar Niemeyer,* 23.

8. Niemeyer, quoted in *The Work of Oscar Niemeyer,* 39.

9. This tradition is as vigorous today as it was sixty years ago, as we may judge from the most recent works of Paulo Mendes da Rocha, among others.

10. For Niemeyer's account of the relationship between their two proposals for the UN, see the summation of his work published as Oscar Niemeyer, *My Architecture* (Rio de Janeiro: Editoria Revan, 2000), 24–29.

11. Le Corbusier, *Oeuvre Complète, 1957–65* (Zurich: Les Editions 'Architecture), 10.

12. Francisco Bullrich, *New Directions in Latin American Architecture* (London: Studio Vista, 1969), 24.

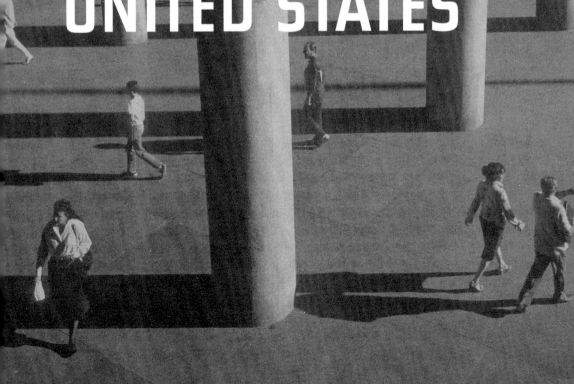

ARCHITECTURE, URBANISM, AND THE GOOD NEIGHBOR POLICY: BRAZIL AND THE UNITED STATES

LAURO
CAVALCANTI

Lucio Costa, Oscar
Niemeyer, Affonso Reidy,
Carlos Leão, Jorge
Moreira, Ernani
Vasconcelos, and
Le Corbusier (consultant),
Ministry of Education
and Health,
Rio de Janeiro,
1937–43.

The birth of the modern style has often been described in terms of the influence of European architects, who had a renewing impact on the Americas, especially French-Swiss Le Corbusier in Brazil and Mies van der Rohe and Walter Gropius in the U.S. Without discounting this approach, I believe that Europe-Americas was not the only axis of influence on modern architecture at that time. Certain exchanges between the United States and Brazil were very important, in the Brazilian case for the internal consolidation of the modern style, for its development vis-à-vis the initial European models, and for its worldwide diffusion. It seems to me that considering a triangulation between the U.S., Brazil, and Europe in the study of the relationship between architecture, art, culture, and political institutions may cast a new light on this complex and fascinating moment.

No European of established reputation, like Mies, Gropius, or Breuer, settled in Brazil, as they did in the United States. Brazil was, however, one of the countries in which the dictates of official French taste in architecture had been dominant since the beginning of the nineteenth century. It is not surprising, therefore, that in its early stages, Brazilian modern architecture had a French accent, especially with Corbusier as a consultant on the Ministry of Education in Rio de Janeiro. Unlike other South American countries at this time, whose buildings were closer to Gropius's ideal of an impersonal, anonymous architecture, Brazil was, in the words of Henry-Russell Hitchcock, "the center of activity of the most intensely personal talent in architecture, Oscar Niemeyer." Indeed, his language exerted considerable influence on his peers and led to the creation of a national language, freed from the constraints of rational functionalism.

In many of its technical aspects, the development of Brazilian architecture owed a great deal to U.S. standards of plumbing and elevators in tall structures. On the other hand, certain structures were designed by North American architects, such as Harrison & Abramovitz's embassy in Rio, or the plan for the City of Motors by José Lluís Sert and Paul Lester Wiener. In the 1930s Santos Maia, one of the most active architects in Rio, designed several buildings in a style that became known as "Manhattan style." Inspired by the skyscrapers in New York, where the architect had lived for three years, his buildings were very successful among entrepreneurs in Rio. Despite the obvious American influence in the Manhattan style, the major contribution of the United States was of a different order: it encouraged Brazilian architects to keep a distance from the European canons through the recognition of the importance of their work, mainly with the *Brazil Builds* exhibition at the Museum of Modern Art in New York and its accompanying catalog. This gave Brazilian modern architecture worldwide exposure that otherwise would not have come so quickly.

By the 1940s modernism was already consolidated as the dominant national style in Brazil. Modern large-scale buildings were constructed in Brazil during this decade, while in war-stricken Europe, architecture was hardly a primary consideration. Meanwhile, the United States, still without any dominant trend in its architectural scene, was the stage for various stylistic experiments after the war. From the early 1950s on, the modernism that the Americas had imported from Europe earlier became a more pluralistic style and traveled the Atlantic in the opposite direction.

In Brazil, Getúlio Vargas was in office from 1930 to 1945 and again from 1951 to 1954. He set about modernizing the country through state initiatives. In his foreign policy, Vargas vacillated between the Axis and the Allies, attempting to garner economic and political benefits from both sides before joining the war on the Allies' side.

The architectural atmosphere was very lively in Brazil because of the competition among modernists, neocolonialists, and academics for the privilege of defining the shapes of the numerous ministerial and other public buildings. Vargas intended to change the

M. M. M. Roberto,
Brazilian Press Association,
Rio de Janeiro,
1936–38.

Oscar Niemeyer,
Chapel at the Palace of Dawn,
Brasilia,
1956–58.

Gregori Warchavchik,
Modernist House,
São Paolo,
1930.

Lucio Costa, Oscar Niemeyer,
Affonso Reidy, Carlos Leão,
Jorge Moreira, Ernani Vasconcelos,
and Le Corbusier (consultant),
Ministry of Education and Health,
Rio de Janeiro,
1937–43.

Lina Bo Bardi,
Bardi Residence,
São Paolo,
1949–51.

Flavio de Carvalho,
group of houses,
São Paolo,
1933–38.

face of the national capital, Rio de Janeiro. Since Brazil was undergoing something of an economic boom, it attracted the interest of architects like Alfred Agache, Marcello Piacentini, and Le Corbusier, who had still not found an opportunity to build on a large scale in Europe.

In the United States, the Good Neighbor Policy was in effect. The year 1940 saw the founding of the Office of the Coordination of Inter-American Affairs (OCIAA), under Nelson Rockefeller's inspiration and command, aimed at extending U.S. political and economic influence over all of Latin America, with special attention to countries like Brazil that had trade partnerships with the Axis.

One problem was the terrible image most of the U.S. population had of Latins, and vice versa, as revealed by a Gallup poll. To overcome this obstacle, Hollywood stars traveled to Latin America as "ambassadors" seeking to attract "opinion makers" from these countries with programs for visits and scholarships to the United States. Meanwhile, activities were planned to show U.S. citizens the positive facets of Latin American countries.

For Brazilians, the main activities included further encouragement for Carmen Miranda's budding Hollywood career and Walt Disney's fifteen-day visit to Rio de Janeiro, resulting in three films and a new character, Joe Carioca. He was a stylized parrot that began to appear with Donald Duck, the two of them personifying what "good neighbors" were expected to be. Franklin Roosevelt sent sculptor Jo Davidson to do busts of Getúlio Vargas and his Latin American peers, while the American press began to replace the usual epithet of dictator with the euphemism "lifetime president." RKO Pictures hired Orson Welles to film *It's All True*, a feature documentary on Brazil, though the project was never completed.

In this essay, I want to analyze two events and their consequences: the design and construction by Oscar Niemeyer and Lucio Costa of the Brazilian pavilion at the New York World's Fair (1939–40) and the Museum of Modern Art traveling exhibition *Brazil Builds* (1943–46). These two episodes involve buildings, events, and institutions that played a major role both in Brazilian and international architectural scenes: The 1939 New York World's Fair was an important place of publicity and propaganda of national cultures, where major architects met and exchanged ideas. By that time, the Department of Architecture and Design of the Museum of Modern Art in New York was becoming the most influential center for the exhibition and diffusion of modern architecture.

In January 1943 the Museum of Modern Art inaugurated in New York the traveling exhibit *Brazil Builds: Architecture New and Old, 1652–1942*, which would be shown in the next three years in forty-eight American cities. The accompanying book, *Brazil Builds*, displayed in photographs, plans, and models a broad panorama of Brazilian buildings, focusing on older construction, as well as approximately fifty buildings by twenty-three modern architects. It differed completely, therefore, from other initiatives promoted by the OCIAA: it was neither a kitsch stylization of stereotypes of Brazil, as were the Carmen Miranda and Walt Disney films, nor an unfinished project like Welles's film.

The preparatory research for the exhibition was done in Brazil during a six-month visit in 1942 by architect Philip Goodwin, code-signer of the original Museum of Modern Art building, and photographer G. E. Kidder Smith. Bernard Rudofsky, who had lived in Brazil from 1938 to 1941, working as an architect in São Paulo, was of great help in suggesting buildings to be photographed and people to be contacted in Brazil. Goodwin was fascinated by Brazil's architectural modernism, and he organized the first major exhibition to capture the unique link it established between revolutionary forms and the discovery and preservation of buildings from the past. *Brazil Builds* accelerated the victory of Brazilian modernism over other styles, especially given the repercussions back in Brazil of that successful exhibition at New York's Museum of Modern Art.

Echoes of *Brazil Builds* reached the main centers of Europe, where critics and architects alike turned their attention to this sophisticated production from a country whose image had virtually always been associated with tropical folklore. Since the *Brazil Builds* show and book, professional periodicals of United States and Europe—mostly *L'Architecture d'aujourd'hui* in France, *Architectural Review* in England, and *Domus* in Italy—have provided recurrent reports on Brazilian architecture. My research indicates that the European magazines usually published projects that had already appeared in American periodicals. Thus we can deduce that the American publications served as the prime reference for the Europeans regarding Brazilian architecture, confirming the importance of the U.S. role in the worldwide diffusion of Brazilian architecture.

Although it relied on the basic vocabulary of the international movement, the Brazilian pavilion in the 1939 New York World's Fair foretold future trends with the freedom of its ramp, the flexibility of its volumes, and the use of *brises-soleil*, thereby establishing a unique language, already independent of that of Le Corbusier. Together with the Finnish and Swedish pavilions, the Brazilian pavilion excited architecture critics like Giedion: "It is a fact of utmost relevance that our civilization no longer develops from a single center, and that creative work emerges in countries which would otherwise remain provincial, like Finland and Brazil."

The New York International Fair had chosen the theme "Building the World of Tomorrow," stressing the contrast between the democratic world of the Americas and totalitarian, strife-ridden

Gregori Warchavchik,
residential building,
São Paolo,
1939.

Lucio Costa,
residential building at Park Guinle,
Rio de Janeiro,
1948–54.

Bernard Rudofsky,
Arnstein Residence,
São Paolo,
1941.

Europe. Latin American nations flocked to the fair, and the Venezuelan pavilion, a daring glass-cased project by the American firm Skidmore & Owings, housed in its interior the Altar of the Good Neighbor, containing a lock of George Washington's hair that General Lafayette had given to Simón Bolívar.

There was almost as much strife in the architectural arena as there was in politics. An organizing committee was created, composed of proponents of the modern style, notably Lewis Mumford. After a negative reaction from the American Institute of Architects, a new, more conservative committee was set up with a compromise solution: "revivalist" styles were admitted in the state pavilions but were forbidden in the foreign section of the fair.

In Brazil, beginning with the Independence Centennial Fair in 1922, the neocolonial style had been considered the national style par excellence, to be used obligatorily in representing the country internationally. Thus the stance taken by the New York World's Fair in keeping revivalist styles out of the international sector was a major triumph for Brazilian modernists. The Brazilian government sponsored a contest won by Lucio Costa and Oscar Niemeyer with a project presenting innovative curves in concrete. They invited Paul Lester Wiener to design the layout of the show inside the exhibition. Costa and Niemeyer spent nearly a year in New York, making one of the most important buildings of Brazilian modern architecture. The Brazilian pavilion has received little study even to this day, and no attention has been given to the professional contacts made by the two Brazilian architects during their year in the United States.

There is significant evidence of cooperation and contact between American and Brazilian architects in the 1940s. As only two examples, I mention the collaboration of Harrison & Abramovitz and Nicmeyer on the design of the United Nations building, and the involvement of Paul L. Wiener and José Sert with Brazilian architects in the planning of City of Motors in Brazil.

We can also track many stylistic similarities in the 1940s and '50s among the projects of Oscar Niemeyer, Sérgio Bernardes, Wallace Harrison and Max Abramovitz, Matthew Nowicki, Henrique Mindlin, Eero Saarinen, Philip Johnson (some buildings), and Skidmore & Owings. Building a national or Pan-American language was not one of the goals of either North American or Brazilian modern architects, as was the case for the neocolonialists. In spite of this, the similarities in some of their architectural approaches and solutions are evident. They represent, if not a language, at least a common accent—with personal input—in the modernism of both countries at that time.

I believe that a history of modern architecture in the 1940s and '50s should not be written only on the basis of the European influence on the Americas. I think that an approach considering a triangular dialogue could expand and shed new light on the understanding of North American, European, and South American architecture.

One of the main goals of this essay is to contribute, as a case study focusing on Brazil, to the writing of the history of the modern architectural movement from multiple and decentralized perspectives. It may help to establish a comparative methodology that can open a whole range of further possibilities on the studies of the modern movement in architecture.

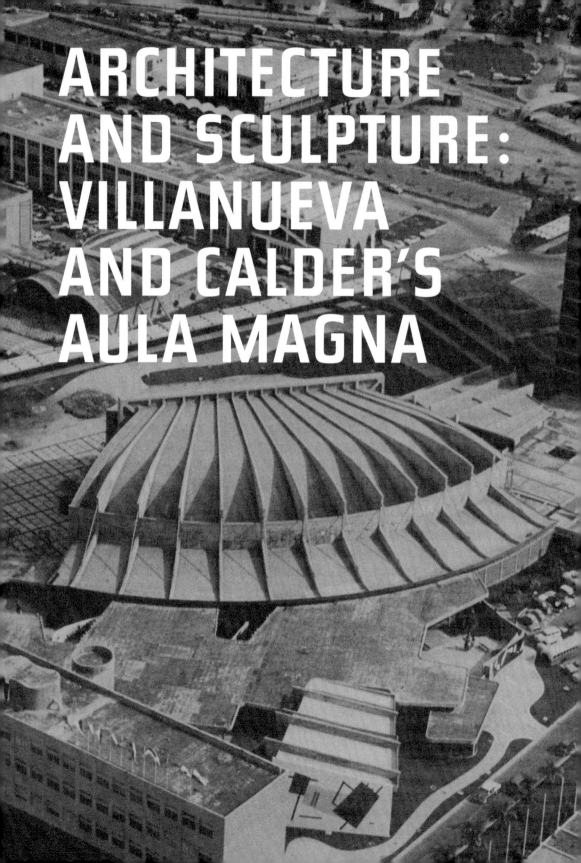

ARCHITECTURE AND SCULPTURE: VILLANUEVA AND CALDER'S AULA MAGNA

CARLOS
BRILLEMBOURG

**One can say that abstract artistic forms have given
great impetus to architecture, although in an indirect
manner. One cannot deny the influences from each
side; architects have also had great influence on
the progress of abstract art. They have held out their
hands in mutual help.**

ALVAR AALTO

Central University of
Venezuela, Caracas.
Aerial view.

The golden period for Latin America's modern architecture began in
September 1929, when Le Corbusier was invited to lecture in Buenos
Aires, Montevideo, and Rio de Janeiro. By the time Le Corbusier returned
to Brazil in 1936 to work with Lucio Costa and his team of young
architects—Oscar Niemeyer, Affonso Reidy, and Jorge Moreira—on
the University City and the Ministry of Education, modern architecture
had already taken hold throughout Brazil, Argentina, and Uruguay. For
a brief period from 1939 to 1959, the work of architects in Brazil,
Uruguay, Argentina, Venezuela, and Mexico was at the vanguard of
the modern movement, which was so sadly interrupted in Europe and
North America by World War II.

In Venezuela, wealth from newly discovered oil brought
architecture to the forefront of a rapidly developing society, and it was
the work of Villanueva that established a role for modern architecture.
Carlos Raúl Villanueva was born in London in 1900. His father, a
diplomat, had represented the governments of both Venezuela and
Nicaragua. In 1928, after finishing his studies at the Ecole des Beaux-

Arts in Paris, the young Villanueva arrived in Caracas for the first time, speaking only rudimentary Spanish, and decided to pursue an architectural career in Venezuela. He spent most of his professional life working on public projects for various government agencies.

In the early 1950s, when Villanueva was at work on the University City, Caracas was no longer a rural colonial city but a modern world capital. Architects such as Gio Ponti, Richard Neutra, Oscar Niemeyer, Roberto Burle-Marx, and Wallace Harrison were at work on major commissions.

The Modernization of Caracas, 1936–58

In the late 1920s Venezuela's economy changed from an agrarian economy, mostly based on coffee, sugar, and cacao, to an exploitative mining economy, following the discovery of large deposits of petroleum in Lake Maracaibo. By 1936 Venezuela's new wealth allowed the government to hire the French architect and urbanist Maurice Rotival to study ways of "modernizing" the urban structure of Caracas. Rotival proposed creating a new Haussmann-esque boulevard by expropriating twelve city blocks. This proposed project divided one of the original colonial squares down the middle with a boulevard lined with new buildings for the new institutions of the regime on the narrow leftover lots. The boulevard was anchored at one end with a grandiose Boullée-type monument to Bolívar carved from the rock in the Parque del Calvario, a prominent hill that dominates downtown Caracas.

In 1941 Carlos Raúl Villanueva's winning design for the El Silencio redevelopment competition proposed reinforcing the existing *calle este-oeste* and ignored Rotival's central axis. He won the competition but was subsequently forced to accept Rotival's axis. The first perimeter housing block that was built did away with the possibility of open axis to the Calvario promontory found in Maurice Rotival's proposal.

This was the first example of large-scale urban renewal and a public housing project in Latin America. This set of buildings is the first important built work of Venezuelan modern architecture. Using the typology of the perimeter block with commercial galleries on the street and private courtyards on the interior, El Silencio remains to this day one of the best examples of urban renewal in a city center.

University City 1944–70

In 1944 the government of General Isaías Medina Angarita purchased the Ibarra sugar plantation and began to build the new Universidad

Carlos R. Villanueva,
El Silencio redevelopment,
Caracas,
1941–45.

Maurice Rotival,
plan for central Caracas,
1938.

Carlos R. Villanueva,
El Silencio redevelopment,
Caracas,
1941–45.

Aula Magna,
Central University of Venezuela,
Caracas.
Access corridor.

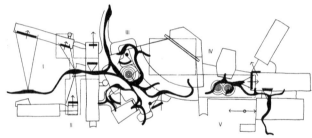

University Campus of Caracas.
Covered plaza and walkways,
1952–53.

Carlos R. Villanueva,
Central University of Venezuela, Caracas,
1952–53.
Circulation flow plan.

Carlos R. Villanueva,
Central University of Venezuela, Caracas,
1952–53.
Covered plaza.

Central de Venezuela on the site. The first axial master plan begins with the construction of the University Hospital in a symmetrical arrangement of buildings along a central axis—a hybrid of the American campus style with a Beaux-Arts central axis. In 1952 the plan was radically changed: the central axis was replaced by a more organic plan featuring a multifocal urbanism.

The luminous *chiaroscuro* of the covered plaza, which serves as a lobby to the Aula Magna theater, the rectory, and the library, is the centerpiece of the new plan. The precedent for this covered plaza is clearly Le Corbusier's lobby in the Palace of the Soviets project, of 1931. All of the covered walks, in particular the covered plaza, are essential connecting elements that give coherence to the open-ended and informal juxtaposition of buildings in the lush tropical landscape of Ciudad Universitaria. Villanueva took to heart Corbu's dictum Architecture Is Circulation.

The covered plaza's fluid space, with carefully screened tropical light, serves as a lobby for the theater and the rectory, as well as a space of quiet meditation filled with the work of artists such as Francisco Narváez, André Bloc, Oswaldo Vigas, Armando Barrios, Baltazar Lobo, Carlos Gonzales Bogen, Alexander Calder, Antoine Pevsner, and Jesús Soto. Villanueva speaks of the importance of artists informing the work of architects, and he put into practice his idea about the synthesis of the arts. In his view, architecture is internal and external, sculpture and also painting. There exists a precise identity for each plastic art, but they all come together to reinforce the position of architecture, at the top of the hierarchy.

Aula Magna 1952–54

Villanueva first saw Calder's sculpture in the Spanish pavilion designed by José Lluis Sert for the 1937 Paris World's Fair, where Villanueva and his contemporary, Luis Malausena, were the architects of the Beaux-Arts Venezuelan pavilion. Villanueva finally met Calder at his studio in Roxbury in 1951; during that visit, Villanueva bought his first Calder mobile, which hangs to this day in his house, Caoma, in Caracas. Discussion began on the University project in 1952, and by June 28 of that year Calder sent a letter stating the conditions for his collaboration on the Aula Magna project. Calder then proposed to work inside the auditorium and not, as Villanueva had suggested, in the covered plaza.

June 28, 1952: Proposal Alexander Calder to Villanueva
I will undertake to make all drawings of the ceiling and the walls of the aula magna—at a scale which will be convenient for you. I will indicate the

colors, which are to be used on the seats and on the floor as well.

I will indicate the lights to be used on the decoration and also those for the general lighting of the hall.

I will consult with Mr. Newman of MIT as to what materials I can use so as to interfere in no way with the acoustics.

For this you are to pay me $5,000 (US)

1000 now
2000 on the delivery of the drawings
2000 by March 1, 1953[1]

Calder did not believe that their *platillos voladores* (floating clouds) would ever be built, and he said to Villanueva that if he managed to build the theater as designed, he was not a man but a devil.... And so his nickname El Diablo was born. Calder himself would not see the Aula Magna until August 15, 1955, when he exhibited his sculptures at the Museo de Bellas Artes. He spent one month working in the metal shop of the university and sold all of the works in the show to Venezuelan collectors. This was when Villanueva became Calder's agent in Caracas, responsible for the sale of various works to Venezuelan collectors such as the historian and photographer Alfredo Boulton, who wholeheartedly embraced Calder's abstract sculpture. Thus a lifelong friendship was formed between the artist and the architect.

During my stay, Carlos had arranged for me to work in the metal shop of the university, and I made two large mobiles, among others. In my show at the Museo de Bellas Artes, everything was sold, most of it right after the opening, and I even had to send some more objects to Caracas when I got home in Roxbury. It is the only time I witnessed a complete sellout of a whole show, and it was also in complete contrast to my last show at Valentin's gallery.[2]

For the Aula Magna, the collaboration was between an architect, a sculptor, and acoustic consultants Bolt Beranek and Newman. The role of the acoustic engineers was essential in determining, together with Calder, the exact angle and the shapes of the acoustical devices.

In record time of five months the Christiani & Nielsen Engineering Firm [the Danish firm that had built the Olympic Stadium] [created] 691 concrete piles, each 18 meters long; [these] were driven into the ground and all the concrete work on the reinforced frame with hollow brick infill completed. A 100-ton steel structure was installed for the ceiling, suspended from 12 inverted L-columns placed fan-like from a transverse frame of 43.75 M span, and supporting a hung plaster ceiling in the interior. Poured in concrete, the roof forms an 8cm-thick planar slab, curving down into a cylindrical shell at the lower rim.[3]

Alexander Calder and Carlos R. Villanueva,
Venezuela,
1955.

Aula Magna.
Interior view during construction.

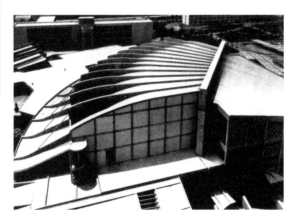

Aula Magna.
Exterior view.

Aula Magna and covered plaza.
Cross section.

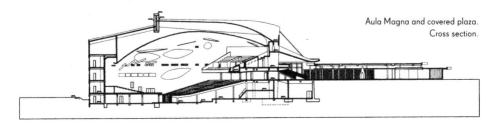

Alexander Calder,
Goldfish Bowl,
1929.

Alexander Calder,
sketch,
1952.

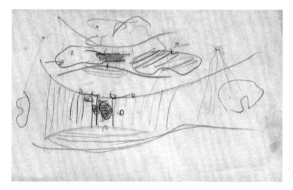

Alexander Calder,
sketch,
1952.

Alexander Calder,
sketch,
1952–53.

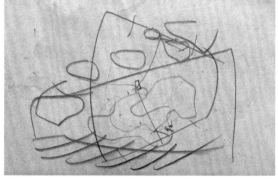

A New Circular Space

Modulating the space acoustically and artistically, the architect discovered a space that is not Corbusian but one that transforms the usual rectilinear perspective into a spherical form very much in line with the aquatic landscape metaphor that Calder and Villanueva had in mind. In Frank Lloyd Wright's Guggenheim Museum (1948–58), we find a spiral and ramped, curved space that also challenged the conventions of the "rectilinear framework" to such an extent that many New York artists signed a manifesto protesting its construction.

Calder's mechanical aquarium, of 1929, is an important precedent for the Aula Magna. The metaphor of an underwater seascape is evident in both the section drawing as a fish with a red eye and in the general plan of the quarter-sphere theater. This motif is carried through in the coral-colored carpet and the golden woolen fabric of the seats, as well as the brilliant, almost tropical colors chosen by Calder for the acoustic "clouds." Later Calder would speak of the Aula Magna as one of his favorite works, calling it "a universe, i.e., spheres of different sizes, densities, colors, and speeds floating in space by means of clouds, rivers, currents of air, viscosities, and smells in the greatest variety and disparity." [4]

The fan-type plan for this 2,600-seat multipurpose auditorium was not the first choice of the acoustic engineers. They had recommended a classical rectangular layout for a concert hall of this size. According to the acoustic engineers who reviewed the plans before Calder got involved:

This auditorium in the shape of a fan is not so appropriate for concerts. We understand that there will be many other uses besides concerts for the auditorium and that it is preferable because of this that it keeps its fan shape. Because of this we will recommend the use of some lightweight reflective surfaces for the lateral walls. For the ceiling, the ideal would be to have reflective surfaces of different sizes and orientations. [5]

Acoustically, the adjustable hanging wooden "clouds" are essential to control the sound and reduce the reverberation. Calder and Newman determined the general form and the placement of the "flying saucers" during several meetings in the offices of Bolt Beranek and Newman.

Calder's mechanical genius, coupled with the guidance of the acoustical consultants, combined in Villanueva's spherical and ludic space to result in a new circular space that is at once multifocal, abstract, and narrative.

Architecture and Sculpture

The appropriation of artistic objects by architects and of architectonic ones by artists is a common occurrence today, as is the confusion about what is architecture and what is sculpture. Architects such as Frank Gehry and Daniel Libeskind make architecture that looks like sculpture, and artists such as Andrea Zittel and Rachel Whiteread make art that looks like architecture. In this project, the sculpture and the architecture are one and the same. A true synthesis of the arts is created by the perfect intertwining of the acoustics, the sculpture, and the space. Although much of the art in the university was integrated with the buildings, some pieces were installed as independent objects.

The collaboration between Villanueva, Newman, and Calder was a linear process: Villanueva determined the space and form of the architectural shell as a fanlike structure with a radial space. The acoustic engineer analyzed the space and suggested the use of a secondary interior shell that would modulate the sound as a broken field of wooden sound baffles, creating a different acoustic space. Calder follows these guidelines and proposed a particular arrangement for the wooden forms, which are hung on cables and angled according to the acoustic principles. In his words: "I had to collaborate with them [Bolt Beranek and Newman] and had to redraw the whole layout all over, once or twice, for Carlos. Newman kept saying, 'The more of your shapes, the merrier and the louder.'"[6]

Three Disciplines: Architecture, Sculpture, and Acoustics

In his autobiography, Calder recalled his collaboration on the Aula Magna thus:

So we drew round and oval shapes some thirty feet or so long, painted different colors and hung from the ceiling with cables from winches. There were also some of these shapes on the sidewalls. When John Foster Dulles attended the tenth Inter-American Conference, he was photographed with a big black triangle on the end of his nose.[7]

Villanueva designed the radial concrete structure that defines the architecture. On the exterior, the structure is the protagonist. The main cross beam that carries the subordinate radial beams acts like a giant concrete canopy. The acoustic consultant determined the need for a secondary acoustic shape within the main shell—a fragmented shell within the main space that efficiently resolves the inherent acoustic problems of this fan-type layout. The artist then proposed some shapes, strictly following the acoustic guidelines.

The overall effect of this spatial experience is not unlike the all-over composition of a painting by Jackson Pollock. Calder's work at this time was marked by the influence of not only Piet Mondrian but also surrealism, as in the work of Joan Miró. The large wooden acoustical panels are perceived in the context of the radial shell of the auditorium and transmit the visual animation of the acoustical properties in such a way as to create the sensation of movement by means of the optical nature of visual mechanics. Villanueva did not believe in the Roman concept of a tabula rasa. Rather than a clean slate, the Aula Magna is more akin to the Hindu concept of *rasa*, as in "a plane of essences."

Exploiting the eye's ability to focus within a curved space, the bifocal parallax mechanism that allows for the perception of distance is challenged by this fish-eye effect and by the strong interaction of color in the floating sculptural objects. To increase this spatial effect, Calder and Villanueva calibrated the lighting of the space. The lighting outlines and projects the "flying saucers" into the space below. Historian Juan Pedro Posani points out that the space expands and contracts, shifts its center of gravity from one end of the hall to the other, submerging the spectator in a perceptive oceanic tension, where the forms link the spectacle and the audience.[8] In contrast to the modulated grid of the mosquelike covered plaza, the inside of the Aula Magna is polymorphous and anti-perspectival. In Villanueva's own words:

Today's epoch insists on the thesis that the only legitimate values for architecture are spatial values. To take possession of a space is the first gesture of all living things, of plants, of clouds, and of men: it is a manifestation of duration, life and equilibrium. Forms may disappear, systems and structures as well, new materials and new techniques appear every day: those who think that modern architecture will resolve their problems with new techniques and new materials are completely mistaken: what is of value, and the only truly new element in today's architecture, is the real and conscious conditioning of space.[9]

Carlos Raúl Villanueva's Legacy Today: A New Conception of Space

Villanueva's work is important not just as a regional reference for Venezuelan architects. The Aula Magna and the Plaza Cubierta, while paying homage to Le Corbusier's definition of architecture as circulation and as the play of forms in light, propose a new conception of space. In the diagrams that he used for teaching architecture, Villanueva named this new type of space a "four-dimensional element." He incorporated

Elevation of Aula Magna, library, and covered plaza,
Central University of Venezuela, Caracas.

Aula Magna, interior view.
Photo by Paolo Gasparini.

the notion of time as a concrete element of space. The spectator inside the Aula Magna senses a radical way of shaping space that corresponds to a multifocal visuality on the one hand and to an animistic conception of form on the other.

This new synthesis can be regarded as fortuitous yet inevitable. Here, we find a moment in architecture's history when an architect and a sculptor not only collaborated on the task at hand but challenged each other's conception of the role of art in society. They also probed the extent of their commitment to a shared view of what art is and what role it plays in architecture. This shared view is much bigger than architecture or sculpture alone and is centered on the life-giving nature of architecture itself.

The client for this project was the State, which allocated the funds necessary to complete this vision because it believed in the destiny of Venezuela as a modern, industrial, developed nation. The cultural renovation implicit in this design was not clearly understood by the government of Marcos Pérez-Jiménez, yet the Aula Magna's flying saucers/clouds have been witnessed by many international political figures, including John Foster Dulles and Fidel Castro. Villanueva understood that, at its best, architecture could be a tool for social betterment, cultural renovation, and urban transformation.

Notes

1. Alexander Calder, letter to Carlos Villanueva, June 28, 1952. Calder Correspondence, Villanueva Foundation, Caracas.

2. Alexander Calder with Jean Davidson, *Calder, An Autobiography with Pictures* (New York: Pantheon Books, 1966), 242.

3. Sibyl Moholy Nagy, *Carlos Raul Villanueva y la Arquitectura de Venezuela* (Caracas: Editorial Lectura, 1964), 119.

4. Alexander Calder, "Manuscript for the Calder Exhibition, September 11–25, 1955, Caracas: Museum of Fine Arts." Correspondence, Villanueva Foundation, Caracas.

5. Bolt Beranek and Newman, "Ciudad Universitaria: Aula Magna." Correspondence, Villanueva Foundation, Caracas

6. Calder, *Calder: An Autobiography with Pictures*, 240.

7. Ibid., 240, 242.

8. William L. E. Perez-Oramas, Niño editors, "Un Moderno en Sudamerica" (Caracas: Galeria de Arte Nacional, 1999), 154.

9. Carlos Raúl Villanueva, "Conference II," *Tendencies in Contemporary Architecture,* Villanueva Foundation, June 13, 1963.

BRILLEMBOURG

ABSTRACTION, ARCHITECTURE, AND THE "SYNTHESIS OF ARTS" DEBATES IN THE RIO DE LA PLATA, 1936–1956

Golden Years

Joaquín Torres García,
gravesite made of
pink granite,
1967,
from a 1935 painting
titled *Estvuctura,*
Montevideo.

The architectural climate in Argentina underwent a renaissance in the late 1930s and '40s. Despite (or because of) the very peculiar political situation, personified by Juan and Eva Perón, the country's economy expanded rapidly. A strong faith in the future colored the expectations and the imagination of everyone in the field of architecture, from construction workers, draftsmen, and foremen, to architects themselves.

European visitors to Argentina were caught up in the excitement as well. For example, in 1948, Marcel Breuer built a restaurant in Mar del Plata. Enrico Tedeschi and Cino Calcaprina, two brilliant Italian architects of his generation, immigrated to Argentina that same year. In 1947 Knoll Associates started the production of the BKF (Butterfly) chair, created by the Argentines Jorge Ferrari Hardoy and Juan Kurchan, with the Catalan émigré Antonio Bonet. Bonet also collaborated with José Lluis Sert on the Spanish pavilion at the 1937 World's Fair in Paris. And in 1949 Le Corbusier broke ground on one of his only two buildings on the American continent: the Curutchet House in La Plata.

Other recent European visitors included the Italian urbanist Giorgio Piccinato, who in the late 1940s stayed in the province of Buenos Aires, where he planned several urban settlements. From the same country of origin, Ernesto La Padula, the very well known creator of the Palazzo della Civiltà Italiana in the EUR neighborhood of Rome, came to the province of Cordoba. And in the early 1950s Marco Zanuso was in Buenos Aires to build the Olivetti factory.

In 1947 the plan that Le Corbusier had prepared for Buenos Aires was adopted by the municipal authorities. Ernesto Rogers, secretary of the CIAM and member of the BBPR group in Milan, collaborated on these studies and taught in the recently created Architecture Institute at the University of Tucumán. In addition to its pedagogic function, the institute was in charge of the University Campus project, a huge building plan of eighteen thousand hectares (almost the same surface area as the entire Federal District), whose complex structures were calculated and tested by Pier Luigi Nervi.[1]

Obviously, the situation in Uruguay cannot be compared with that of Argentina. Aside from the differences in dimension (Uruguay is roughly one-sixteenth the size of Argentina), there are also substantial distinctions in their economic structures, political histories, and cultural traditions. Nevertheless, in spite of its small size, the artistic and architectural life of Uruguay was surprisingly rich during this period. Uruguay was a stable, educated, wealthy nation with the best standard of living in Ibero-America and with the most informed people (highest literacy rates; greatest quantity of newspapers, radios, and television sets; highest sales of books per inhabitant). Although these conditions did not yield architectural consequences as spectacular as those found in Argentina, it was during this period that the most magnificent parts of Montevideo were built. With its homogeneous high-quality urban front, the Rambla República del Perú, in the Pocitos neighborhood, is a wonderful expression of these glory days. Moreover, it was at this time that Antonio Bonet built his extraordinary works on the beaches of La Solana del Mar.[2]

Optimism and self-confidence did not last long, however. An indepth analysis of the political and economic changes goes beyond the scope of the present essay, but the fact is that most of the Italians mentioned above returned to their country, the office of the Buenos Aires plan was dismantled, the University Campus in Tucumán was never finished, and the majority of the major projects mentioned above were never built.

I will present here what I consider to be a remarkable set of architectural projects and ideas related to these golden years of cultural richness and self-confidence on both sides of the river. I will show these projects, ideas, and figures in light of the particular debates on nonfigurative art because these debates set the agenda in those days and because they also included architectural culture, owing to the great interest in the "synthesis of arts."

Abstract Art in the Rio de la Plata

The Rio de la Plata does not have a particularly rich tradition in the visual arts. Impressionism, fauvism, expressionism, and even surrealism had a delayed reception. There were some significant figures—Pedro Figari and Rafael Barradas in Uruguay, Emilio Pettoruti and Xul Solar in Argentina. But compared with the importance and originality of the region's literary creations (from the pens of the Uruguayan-born Comte de Lautreamont and Argentine Jorge Luis Borges, among others), it can be said that local painting and sculpture lacked cultural consistency in the first decades of the twentieth century.

One of the most relevant figures in the twentieth-century fine arts scene in this region was Joaquín Torres García. Born in 1876 in a small Uruguayan town, he spent most of his life abroad, returning to his country in 1934. A pioneer of modernism, he, along with neoplasticists Piet Mondrian and Theo van Doesburg, considered abstraction to be the highest expression of the human spirit. But he disagreed with those artists in that he considered theirs a purely geometric exercise that ignored the communicative function of art. Torres García believed that by incorporating symbols into his work, he had found an abstract way to respond to that demand.[3]

The aim of the artist, he believed, should be to "build" his work, that is, to reduce it to an abstract grid of lines and colors. But, for Torres's monistic conception, it was also possible and necessary to communicate one's own experience through a work of art. By means of this experience, mankind could establish ties with the whole universe in space and time. Torres's central idea of experience, and the search for purity that he shared with members of the avant-garde, had its roots in his trip back to Uruguay. He was searching for a place where a working artistic community could look for a universalistic constructivism rooted in the forgotten abstract cultures of Indo-America: the Escuela del Sur would be his project.[4] Torres's exceptional personality and art had an enormous impact on both shores of the Rio de la Plata. In Montevideo, the Taller Torres García (TTG), created in 1943, launched the careers of talented artists such as Augusto and Horacio Torres, Julio Alpuy, and Gonzalo Fonseca, among others. Torres and the TTG exerted a powerful influence on architects and students of architecture.[5]

Joaquín Torres García in his studio,
Montevideo,
1934.

Augusto Torres,
mural, Sindicato Medico,
Montevideo,
1954.

Gonzalo Fonseca,
concrete tower,
Mexico City,
1967–68.

The first manifestation of nonfigurative avant-garde work in Buenos Aires occurred in 1933 with an exhibition of the work of Juan del Prete.[6] Nonfigurative art became a trend in 1944 with the publication of *Arturo* magazine, a manifesto for concrete art. Torres was certainly an influential intellectual mentor of this movement, but he was not the only one. Dutch and Swiss concrete artists such as Theo van Doesburg, Sophie Tauber, Georges Vantongerloo, Friedrich Vordemberge-Gildewart, and especially Max Bill were also very important references for many members of the group, which disbanded after the short-lived *Arturo* magazine closed down. As a result, in 1945 the Asociación Arte Concreto-Invención was founded under the leadership of Tomás Maldonado, and in 1946 the Grupo Madí appeared, with Gyula Kosice as its most active figure.[7] Both groups were opposed to all manner of metaphysics, figuration, existentialism, and sentimentalism. They proclaimed that the artist should concentrate on a cool, scientific organization of his own specific materials. For this reason, they refused the idea of "creation" and instead adopted the concept of "invention" as a radicalized version of Torres's "construction."

Madí gave priority to an investigation of the spatial effects of artistic materials. The group employed bright colors and bold geometric forms: circles, spheres, waves, arches, spirals, and stripes dominate their compositions. According to their publications, "Madí painting [is] colour and bidimensionality. Cut away and irregular frame, flat surface and curve and concave surface. . . . Madí sculpture, tridimensionality, not colour. Total form and solids with contour, and articulation, rotation and translation motions, etc. Madí architecture, mobile and shiftable environment and form." [8]

The question of space was at the center of the debates in the visual arts milieu in Buenos Aires during this period. In 1946 Lucio Fontana presented his *Manifesto Bianco* (White Manifesto), which advocated a "spatialist" art involving the fourth dimension. In 1951 Bruno Zevi gave lectures on his phenomenological, Crocian theories of architectural space for an enormous audience at the School of Law of the University of Buenos Aires. Moreover, exiled Spanish republican Jorge Oteiza was also in Buenos Aires, beginning his research on minimalism.

For his part, Maldonado criticized Torres for his use of symbolism and especially for the use of shadows in his canvases. For Maldonado, these shadows were a technical tool that represented an unacceptable return to naturalism. Moreover, following Max Bense's technological aesthetics, he rejected the creation of any kind of "style" as formal system. For Torres, art should approach science and concentrate on the application of a method. Paraphrasing Bill, Maldonado wrote, "A form organizes itself according to its own 'law of development' and taking as a starting point its own inner data. It is from the dialectics of form, from its peculiar manner of being born, and never from preestablished proportional or harmonic outlines, that methods of structuration must be inferred."[9]

Architecture and the "Synthesis of Arts"

The agenda of art and that of architecture were intertwined in the Rio de la Plata during the first half of the 1940s. A reevaluation of this relationship was important for the traditional architectural establishment, which was still in shock from modernist ideologies. But few could deny that the old academic theories and principles were outdated. Thus, to incorporate "art" into architecture was considered one of the best ways to recuperate the rhetoric of "spiritual values" abandoned under the devastating effects of the radical, functional, and mechanistic revolution.

But the main impulse to articulate the relationship between art and architecture had other, more positive origins. In fact, at least two Latin American events had a strong impact on artists and architects in the Rio de la Plata: the advent of Mexican muralism and of Brazilian modern architecture. With its postulate of a symphonic orchestration of all the arts as revolutionary tools destined for the education of the masses, Mexican muralism got under way in the 1920s. Nevertheless, one can speak of a local movement with the same ideas only after 1933, as a result of the presence in Montevideo and Buenos Aires of Mexican muralist and political activist David Alfaro Siqueiros. Seeking refuge from political prosecutions in his country, Siqueiros spent a short time in Montevideo, where he gave some lectures before being thrown out by the local authorities. In Buenos Aires, a group of Argentine and Uruguayan artists—Spilimbergo, Berni, Castagnino, and Lázaro—collaborated with him on the realization of the mural *Espacio Plastico* and proclaimed the necessity of an urban art in their manifesto.[10] In 1944 they would create a "mural art atelier," with the intention of "develop[ing] mural painting as much as possible in our country, knowing the place that it has in relation to modern architecture."

Integration of the arts was one of the most celebrated qualities of Brazilian modern architecture, as evidenced in the use of applied decoration and the collaborative participation of a team of painters, sculptors, architects, and landscape experts in the creation of Rio de Janeiro's Ministry of Education. The inauguration of the University City in Mexico and the covered plaza in Caracas in the early 1950s gave another boost to this trend, which Henry-Russell Hitchcock would consider a Latin American characteristic because local elites "expect more from architects than purely 'functional' solutions."[11]

Hitchcock was not the only critic who promoted the artistic singularity of "Latin American architecture." Bernard Rudofsky also presented architecture in Latin America as a foil to the increasingly commercialized work in the U.S.[12] But it was Sigfried Giedion who did the most to publicize and endorse the unprejudiced art / architecture enterprises in the region. For Giedion, these ventures demonstrated the possibilities of the "new monumentality" as a response to *Sachlichkeit*, commercialism, and old-fashioned academicism. "The contact between architect and artists," he wrote, "is for artistic development at least as important as the control of climatic devices."[13]

With J. M. Richards, Giedion was the leading figure on the commission that, at the seventh CIAM in Bergamo in 1949, debated the "synthesis of arts" through the "Report on the Plastic Arts." In 1951 Giedion published *A Decade of New Architecture*, giving a central role to Latin Americans, and in the same year he and Le Corbusier played an important role in organizing the São Paulo biennale. Moreover, Giedion and other CIAM leaders cooperated with the International Arts Conference, organized by UNESCO in Venice in 1952.

Mario Payssé-Reyes: Art Everywhere

In the context of the debates mentioned above, the ideas and work of Torres García and his school had a different effect on architecture. Some of the TTG artists conceived and built architectural artifacts, as was the case of Horacio Torres, Rosa Acle, and especially Gonzalo Fonseca. During Torres García's lifetime, the first collaborative enterprise between art and architecture involved the construction of the Saint Bois Hospital in Montevideo: the TTG was invited to paint a series of murals by architects Sara Morialdo and Luis Surraco. Paintings, decorations, murals, and "constructive" furniture integrate the houses of Torres García and his son Horacio Torres. The houses were designed by Ramon Menchaca and Ernesto Leborgne. Leborgne also designed his own house, with the artistic collaboration of Torres García, Matto, Alpuy, and other artists of the TTG.[14]

The relationship between architecture and art was also important for Julio Vilamajó, the most influential Uruguayan architect of this period. As a result of his academic studies, Vilamajó viewed "integration of arts" as a crucial condition of his architectural creations, as is evident in buildings like the eclectic Santa Lucia palace and the Pérsico House of 1926. The same intention can be recognized even in the modernist house he built for himself in 1930, where delicate pieces of ceramic with marine allusions were incorporated to illuminate the facades with colorist effects. Similarly, art was to have a major place

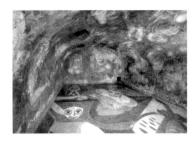

David Alfaro Siqueiros,
Espacio Plasticio,
Buenos Aires,
1944.

Gonzalo Fonseca,
Muro Blanco,
Caracas,
1977.

Horacio Torres,
mural for low-income house by
Mario Payssé-Reyes,
1950.

Julio Vilamajó,
Engineering Faculty,
University of the Republic,
Montevideo,
1937.

in his most important building, the Engineering Faculty, built between 1939 and 1948.

Given these examples, which are based on figurative representations, it could be said that the concept of art / architecture integration in Vilamajó's work had nothing in common with the abstract ideals of Torres and his disciples. It should be noted, however, that in his Engineering Faculty building Vilamajó introduced one of several significant novelties: the exhibition of the structural grid. The impact of Auguste Perret's lectures in Montevideo in 1937 cannot be discounted in explaining this change, but also evident in the presence of the spatial, almost abstract fabric of columns and beams unifying the building's complex composition is the influence of the TTG research on constructivism.[15]

Mario Payssé-Reyes was a student of Vilamajó and inherited his studio at the school of architecture. Vilamajó's influence on Payssé's work is especially evident in buildings like the apartment houses on Roque Graseras Street and Estigarribia Street in Montevideo from 1952 and 1947.[16] Payssé seems to have been a frequent visitor of the TTG, and he was convinced of the importance of what he called "the integration of architecture with the other plastic arts." It should be noted that he did not speak of "synthesis." In fact, Payssé's concept of "integration" had nothing to do with the search for an egalitarian artistic community. On the contrary, he postulated the subordination of "minor" arts to the "major" art of architecture. The architect must be the one to decide where and how the plastic arts can be part of his building. Out of architecture plastic artists are like "loosed children."

This authoritarian conception of "integration" was founded on academic lessons but also on Payssé's understanding of order. He considered all of history to be a succession of calm, classic periods, followed by periods of crisis and instability. During the epochs of agitation and decadence—and ours is one of this kind—human beings' attitudes could be grouped in the two biblical poles of Zelotes and Herodians. "The former believe that the world can achieve order only after each man finds this order within himself. The others [think] that the world must be arranged first, and then within this frame each man can achieve order. The former are philosophers and humanists, the latter technicians, logicians, and social planners."[17]

A conservative man who rejected outright the growing social effervescence in his country, Payssé identified himself with the Zelotian party. In spite of his interest in the postulates of Teilhard de Chardin, he believed that contemporary thought suffered the "vice of scientificism" and that as a result it was necessary "to beat out of science the tree of professions."[18] Because of this way of thinking, Payssé's interest seems to have been concentrated on two main aspects of Torres García's theories and practices. One is the main postulate that separated Torres from Van Doesburg and other neoplasticist artists, namely, the belief in the necessity to include not only "technical" impulses in the work but spiritual ones as well. To insist on artistic implications was a way of "beating out of science" the tree of architecture. Moreover, Payssé shared with Torres (and with Le Corbusier, of course) a strong Pythagorean understanding of the world. The existence of a secret network of rational proportions was a demonstration of a higher will and creativity. Architects, Payssé believed, should try to inscribe their work into these networks of divine perfection.

Payssé's ideas during this period are embodied in the house he built for himself and his family (1953) and in the archdiocesan seminary in Montevideo, conceived in 1954. The house is organized as boxes within a box. The outer box acts as a container that gives order to the organic articulation of the interior. Brick is the main material, but it is used as a closure, and the structure is only partially revealed, clearly negating any "technical" predominance and denying its mainly proportional and rhythmic purpose. Several TTG artists—Elsa Andrada, Augusto Torres, Edwin Studer, Horacio Alpuy, F. Matto Vilaró—collaborated on the paintings, sculptures, and even the design of the table settings for the house.

The seminary is a big complex located on the outskirts of Montevideo. Its functions are organized around various patios. The chapel and the clock tower occupy the main part of the composition. Thanks to the work of Horacio Torres, the complex is probably the most eloquent example of the "integration of arts" in the Rio de la Plata.

Some of the techniques that Payssé employed in his house recur in the seminary: the discriminate use of the structural grid, a heavy reliance on brick, a careful composition, and the application of regulatory layouts. The most surprising feature of the seminary is the supergraphics created by Payssé himself. Even more than the appeal to sculptors and painters, the superimposition of written messages over the architecture appears here as an obvious and desperate admission of the semantic crisis of architecture.

In fact, the building had a short life as a seminary; it later became a school for army officers.[9] With their appeal to "truth," "reason," and "moral," the big brick letters originally evoked the principles of the church and the fights between Zelotes and Herodians. It is difficult to ignore the irony that they were later to mark a rarefied scene for the torture that, according to witnesses, would take place here in the 1960s and '70s.

Mario Payssé-Reyes,
Payssé Residence,
Montevideo,
1953.

Mario Payssé-Reyes,
detail,
Archdiocesan Seminary,
Montevideo.
1954.

Mario Payssé-Reyes,
Archdiocesan Seminary,
Montevideo.
1954.

Architectural Autonomy: From System to Method

On the Argentinean side of the Rio de la Plata, the radical exclusion of any naturalistic representation or, more precisely, of any subordination of the artistic form to systems or stimulus outside its own limits was one of the principles that the abstract artists shared with some modernists architects of the 1940s. An insistence on the work of art as a pure technical artifact and a search for purity were the others.

In spite of the Marxist interpretations of Maldonado and the Madí artists, many architects were fascinated by the ideological freedom afforded by the "technological aesthetic." Paraphrasing Peter Meyer, they recognized in it the basis for "an autonomous art, that is, an art without ties to extra-aesthetic values, [an art that] belongs to the same existential field of science, free of every ethic, and in the end, religious determination." [20] It was in those years and framed by this intellectual climate that Mario Roberto Alvarez, César Janello, Eduardo Catalano, and Amancio Williams began their careers.

Apart from Ernesto Rogers and his BBPR group, Catalano was the only architect whose work was presented at the 1946 *Abstract-Concrete-Non Figurative Art* exhibition in Buenos Aires. His research was characterized by a belief in the centrality of the structure as a key "to build[ing] the eternal for the many presents." [21] One can see here some traces of Torres García's predicament and certainly also of the lessons offered by Perret during his stay in Buenos Aires. The design of the Buenos Aires auditorium for twenty thousand spectators was a technical tour de force inspired by those ideas. But Catalano's rejection of any sign of temporality in his work, along with his interest in "constants," led him to observe and adopt the structural forms of the natural world. This organic structuralism is especially apparent in his house in Raleigh and in his designs for the Santa Maria Stadium and for a skyscraper.

Helio Piñon has observed that, for his part, Alvarez understood "from the beginning the constructive foundation of modern form, its capacity to structure physical reality with criteria of order, and the subordinate status of the figurative in the space of consistency of the artifact." [22] At the beginning of his career, Alvarez was deeply committed to the search for an autonomous architecture strictly subordinated to internal determinations. Between approximately 1947 and 1954, in buildings such as his D'Abrollo House and the Buenos Aires Municipal Theater, he defined the architectural language that, with traces of Mies and Neutra, would characterize his entire production until today. Murals and sculptures populate the theater but not as expressions of any attempt at artistic synthesis. Rather, they are treated as simple additions according to the program of a building that for many years would house the Museum of Contemporary Arts. Despite their very different conceptions of autonomy, Catalano and Alvarez do have something in common: both believed in the necessity of a system. Their architectural ideas constitute a harmonic universe where every piece occupies a calculated position.

This was not true of César Janello and Amancio Williams. Following Giulio Carlo Argan, we could say that, for them, rationality was important not as a "system" but rather as a "method."[23] In fact, although Janello was a disciple of Williams and worked as an architect early in his career, he would excel as a designer and especially as a theoretician.

In his pavilions for the 1952 America's Fair in Mendoza, Argentina, designed with Gerardo Clusellas, he adopted a pure Miesian language but with an accurate use of wood instead of steel. At the abovementioned *Abstract-Concrete-Non Figurative Art* exhibition, Janello's interest in the unification of artistic and useful form was expressed in his W chair. Because of its ties to the simultaneous research by sculptors such as Ennio Iommi and Claudio Girola about the line in space, but also because of its unsolved problems, the W chair can be considered an end and a beginning. As Alejandro Crispiani pointed out, Janello's piece shows how problematic it was to extend to the useful and practical the existence of a "white function" of art, "its property of producing beauty departing from a 'gay technique' that embodied its ludic content."[24] Thus, in spite of other valuable projects and buildings he produced in the following years, Janello's career was more and more guided by the search for objective basements for the architectural form. His work in this field was intense and achieved its highest expression in the creation, at the University of Buenos Aires, of the world's first chair of architectural semiology in 1968, and a decade later of his internationally recognized Theory of Spatial Delimitation.[25]

But the search for a common method for art and design products based on an objective arrangement of the inherent technical data, without any type of applied illusion or external input, found its most acute expression in the work of Amancio Williams.[26] To this period belong the House over the Brook (1943), the Houses in Space (1942–43), the Buenos Aires airport (1945), the hospitals in Corrientes, the Suspended Office Building (1946), the floating sanitation stations, the houses in Munro and Pereyra Iraola, the gas station, and the theater for sound and space shows (1943–53).

An examination of four of Williams's projects will highlight the main characteristics of his work. The House over the Brook, located in a densely wooded site in Mar del Plata, was conceived as a holiday residence for the architect's father. Williams set out to raise the house

Amancio Williams,
House over the Brook,
Mar del Plata,
1943.

Amancio Williams,
detail of stairs at House
over the Brook.

César Janello and Geraldo Clusellas,
pavilion for America's Fair,
Mendoza, Argentina,
1952.

off the ground but also to eliminate columns; thus, the structure was designed like a bridge. Its main characteristics are: (1) total liberation of the ground; (2) respect for the existing trees, and therefore the use of the unique disposable free surface, crossed by the brook; (3) use of a gallery plan, typical in the Pampean plains; (4) a free volume in space supported by the elegant curve of a bridge vault (the house in space replicates an airplane profile); (5) a bridge that mirrors the natural shape of the site; (6) obsessively perfect construction.

The theater, officially known as the Hall for Visual Spectacle and Sound in Space, is one of his most perfect architectural theorems. The challenge was to create a six-thousand-seat theater, suitable for any kind of modern or traditional performance, with exactly the same perfect acoustic conditions for all spectators, with no more than sixteen lines, without touching the ground. If the House over the Brook re-creates a simple and traditional gallery house, the theater is a reinterpretation of a simple and traditional circus.

The hospitals (1951) were to be located in the hot, humid, subtropical northeast region of Argentina. Following his standard method, Williams conceived a solution beyond time and space. In this case, the solution anticipated the "mat" criteria that would be applied more than ten years later to this kind of building, as seen in particular in Le Corbusier's Venice Hospital. A systematic constitution of the different areas with total freedom for its articulation, as well as the unification of the whole building complex, is achieved by the incorporation of elegant vaults that simultaneously guarantee climate control.

Another theorem: the suspended office building (1946). The question this time was how to obtain maximum free surface, exactly the same, for each one of the whole floors of a skyscraper? The building was to be located in Buenos Aires and was to demonstrate that it was quite possible to liberate the ground floor, to distribute mechanical installations clearly, and to avoid using large quantities of steel (scarce in wartime Argentina). As often happens with scientific theories, Williams's theorem would be proved some decades later.

This exceptional intellectual research should be considered in connection with the cultural climate in which it was produced. Williams knew and admired the work of the concrete artists and was especially close to Maldonado, Lidy Prati, and Iommi. He probably entered the world of the plastic avant-gardists in Buenos Aires through his wife and former partner, Delfina Bunge, who visited the first exhibitions of Emilio Pettoruti with her father, when she was thirteen years old.[27] Amancio's enthusiasm for modern art drove him to buy works of Fernand Léger and Max Bill, whom he met in Europe in 1947. But in spite of the importance of these relationships, it is difficult to establish a direct and unilateral dependence of his ideas. Williams's

Amancio Williams,
Union Industrial Office Building,
1946. Competition entry.

Amancio Williams,
concert hall,
1942–43.

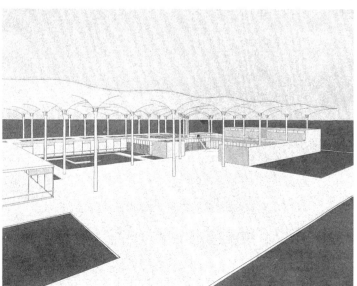

Amancio Williams,
three hospitals in
Corrientes, Argentina,
1948–1953.

House over the Brook was designed in 1943, a year before the publication of *Arturo*, the first magazine on concrete art. Nevertheless, it is clear that Williams's work has to be considered a fundamental episode in the debates around abstract / concrete art and the investigations on unified method. As previously mentioned, this method was based on the idea of invention, and in fact Williams's entire oeuvre can be considered a series of architectural inventions in the most literal sense of the word.

In fact, Williams considered himself essentially an inventor. His father, Alberto Williams, was a composer of nationalist music, and certainly music was an important part of Amancio's education, especially the emphasis on nationalism, which was later reinforced by his father-in-law, Manuel Galvez, a nationalist writer himself and one of the most important intellectuals in Argentina. But Amancio remembered the main figure of his childhood to be not his father but the Spanish gardener/ steward/chauffeur of his house, a problem-solving, spontaneous bricoleur who fascinated the child.

As Beatriz Sarlo has noted, the 1920s and '30s were a propitious time for the culture of invention in Argentina.[28] From the time Williams began studying engineering until his entry into the field of aviation, science and technology occupied a central place in the imagination of Buenos Aires, a city with more than seven weekly magazines dedicated to technical hobbies; radio, photograph, and film technologies; scientific revelations; and amateur invention. Inventors and inventions also occupied an important place in literature, as seen in the work of Horacio Quiroga, Roberto Arlt, and, most notably, Adolfo Bioy Casares, who was the author of the well-known novella *The Invention of Morel* (1940).

Certainly Williams, as a conscious member of the elite, was not interested in domestic mechanics, but rather in airplanes and sophisticated engines. In the 1930s aviation was in a period of institutional organization in Argentina and, as in other Latin American countries under the influence of modernizing military leaders— Marmaduke Grove in Chile, Leonidas Trujillo in Santo Domingo, and Getulio Vargas in Brazil—it enjoyed intense official promotion. Amancio volunteered for the army, which gave him the opportunity to train as a pilot. His enthusiasm for planes led him to create a private aviation company, which he ran for three years.

It was not until 1938 that, as he expressed it in a letter to Le Corbusier, Williams left behind "le tourbillon d'une société décadente" and reorganized his life according to "un très fort désir de chercher la vérité." [29] Brought up by his mother in the Protestant faith, Amancio "discovered" Catholicism through the International Eucharistic Congress, which the Vatican organized in Buenos Aires in 1934, and through the intense religious devotion of his fiancée, Delfina Galvez. He converted to Catholicism at the end of the decade.

It was at this moment that he encountered the conceptual world that would constitute the ideological framework for his research. Paradoxically, his radical search for a concrete architecture exclusively grounded on internal determinants seems to have been initially guided by his religious, moral determination "to seek the truth." In fact, in another letter to Le Corbusier, Williams described his atelier as an active intellectual circle that offered periodical lectures on theology, philosophy, history, and art.[30] Hector Bernardo and Jordán Bruno Genta are the most important figures mentioned in that letter. Both of them were part of the extreme right wing that inspired the pro-Fascist coup d'état in 1943 that installed Juan Perón in his first public position in the national government.

The marriage of avant-garde architecture with nationalist fanaticism and reactionary ideologies should not be surprising. As Jeffrey Herf has shown in the case of Germany: "Reactionary modernists were nationalists that transformed the romantic anti-capitalism of the German Right away from backward-looking pastoralism, pointing instead to the outlines of a beautifully new order, replacing the formless chaos due to capitalism in united and technologically advanced nation." [31] In fact, we can read in Bernardo's writings the same strong critique of liberal past that is present in Williams's rejection of the "chaotic" organization and results of modern industry.

Bernardo, Genta, and other nationalist and Catholic leaders of the 1940s believed that it was first necessary to reestablish a platonic conception of absolute truth, as opposed to liberal "Lutheran" relativism. And it would be a precise "method, similar to the one scientists should apply in order to reach the goal of their investigation, that is, the attainment of truth." [32] Not by chance did Bernardo dedicate chapters of his book on economy to planning. During Perón's rule, Bernardo promoted Williams's plan for Patagonia and the hospitals in Corrientes. Against hybrid attitudes, petty interests, sentimentalism, and all kinds of pragmatism, the national Catholicism of the 1940s recommended heroism, purity, and reason as the best way to act "as God": "Only when one wants to be like God can one remember the divine ascendancy of man." [33]

Thus, paradoxically, to look for absolute truth in this way meant to think "epocally," that is, to create beyond the small particularities and determinations of place and present, projecting the work to the future, precisely to that point when, as a perfect product of reason, this absolute truth would finally be received by its correspondent matter, space, and time.

Eladio Dieste,
Atlántida Church,
Atlántida, Uruguay,
1957–58.

Eladio Dieste,
interior of the Atlántida Church.

Eladio Dieste,
San Pedro de Durazno church,
Montevideo, Uruguay,
1967–71.

Eladio Dieste: The Place Factor

The extraordinary creations of Eladio Dieste are very well known. The Atlántida Church, the San Pedro de Durazno church, the various towers, and the vaults he built for numerous industrial buildings have been widely published in recent years.[34] He is also well known for his preference for brick, the intelligence of his structural solutions, and the respect and importance he gave to the role of the workers in his construction processes. My point is that Eladio Dieste's understanding of reality was very different from Williams's platonic approach. They shared a belief in the technically based autonomy of architecture, and in this sense neither one was interested in any kind of synthesis or integration of arts à la Payssé. The arts could and should have something in common, but an artificial collaboration among practices would not lead to a harmonious world. For Dieste, invention was "inevitable" in order "to be humanly, truly constructing in this world, making it for man."

If Williams was backed by Maldonado's radical theories and by the elitist modernism of his nationalist friends, Dieste was grounded in the new Catholic Latin American movements that postulated the need for a church positioned on the side of the poor. According to him, it was dull to "think in the abstract without direct contact with reality."

In Dieste's writings, art is considered a vehicle for the contemplation of the divine work that is visible in each molecule of reality. His conception of technical work was clearly in line with the principle of *adequatio intelecto et re*, that is, technique understood as a human artifact that emerges from real data.

It is not unusual that these conceptions matured in Dieste's thought in the early 1950s. In 1947 Montevideo was the seat for the first South American meeting of Christian Democrat leaders. The meeting, organized by such people as the Uruguayan leader Dardo Regules and the Chilean Eduardo Frei Montalva (future president of Chile), established the foundations for Christian Democrat parties in the region; this political group would exert an enormous influence over progressive, non-Communist intellectuals in the coming years.

Oriented toward a realistic understanding of the contemporary world, Christian Democrats were mainly inspired by the ideas of philosopher Jacques Maritain and, more generally, a modern interpretation of Thomas Aquinas's thinking. It is within this cultural context that we should consider Dieste's articulation of architecture, science, art, reality, and faith. His devotion to the lower classes and his belief in the social function of art should be related to the call for an "art for the human community"—in opposition to a bourgeois "art for art's sake" and a Communist "art for the people"—as was postulated by Maritain.[35] Moreover, Dieste's love for the rough material condition of architecture can also be tied to Maritain who, quoting Thomas Aquinas in his conferences at Princeton University in 1951, remembered: "The kind of good which art pursues is not the good of the human will or appetite [or the good of man], but the good of the very works done or artifacts." And so, if art was, for Dieste, "the expression—even arbitrarily mysterious due to its media—of consciousness, intense and volatile, of man and the world," for Maritain "poetry [was] necessary, because it brings to men a vision of reality-beyond-reality, an experience of the secret meanings of things, an obscure insight into the universe of beauty, without which men could neither live nor live morally." [36]

Nevertheless, Dieste's strong modernist defense of the "inevitable invention" and his refusal of any kind of folkloric revival of art seem to have been supported by another French Catholic thinker whose ideas were very well diffused in the Rio de la Plata in the 1950s and '60s: Teilhard de Chardin. The influence of Teilhard was not limited to his defense of the unity between scientific methods and Christian beliefs, but also included his understanding of the divinity of matter and his holistic conception of the harmony between man and nature into what Teilhard called the "noosphere." He wrote:

All around us, to the right and left, in front and behind, above and below, we have only to go a little beyond the frontier of sensible appearances in order to see the divine welling up and showing through. But it is not only close to us, in front of us, that the divine presence has revealed itself. It has sprung up universally, and we find ourselves so surrounded and transfixed by it that there is no room left to fall down and adore it, even within ourselves. By means of all created things, without exception, the divine assails us, penetrates us and moulds us. We imagined it as distant and inaccessible, whereas in fact we live steeped in its burning layers. *In eo vivemus.* As Jacob said, awakening from his dream, the world, this palpable world, which we were wont to treat with the boredom and disrespect with which we habitually regard places with no sacred association for us, is in truth a holy place, and we did not know it. *Venite, adoremus.* [37]

Dieste's specific circumstances led to his strongly rooted solutions, in opposition to Williams's research on universal archetypes. And it is in this respect that his "constructive" attitude approaches Torres García's predication for a localized, American art. [38] In contrast to Mondrian's essentialism and acceptance of the heritage of cubism, this localization was, for Torres, a consequence of his interest in experience as the instrument that could reveal the unity of the whole. Universalism could only be achieved through the form of singular expressions of singular states of soul. The artist, he believed, should be the sensible point where the whole present would condense in space, and the whole history in time.

Dieste's rejection of folklorism is very similar to Torres's refusal to mimic Indian art. Moreover, he did not ignore the universal lesson of his austere and unpretentious brick structures. Dieste believed that his technique could compete with more sophisticated solutions in the United States. It was not economy but ideology that separated efficacy from sensibility, that made us see, "for example, a transmission tower [as something] devoid of signification; through it passes all the richness of human life, and its membranes are like ears and mouths." [39]

Dieste conceived of art as the way to recover human harmony for the world, and in this sense he was not far from concretism. As Tomás Maldonado pointed out, "Against the irresponsible fragmentation of culture, Bill opposes the will of coherence, that is, the desire to promote a new and integral method for the interpretation and creation of the visual events of our time, what Bill calls, so very aptly, the 'good form.'" For Dieste, this "good form" was not a direct consequence of industry, design, calculation, or creativity but a manifestation of "piety," that is, of a profound identification with the suffering and joy of the others. As he wrote in *The Conscience of Form*, "If the expressivity of human density were extended to everything we see, art would not be confined to the museums. It would live in the street." [40]

Notes

1. See Jorge Francisco Liernur, *Arquitectura en la Argentina del Siglo XX. La construcción de la modernidad* (Buenos Aires, 2001). For more on the presence of Italian architects in Argentina, see "Papers on Fire: An Attempt of Frustrated Immigration: Italian Architects of the Post World War II and the Architectural Debate in the New Argentina (1947–1951)," by J. F. Liernur, *Metamorfosi* (Rome) 25–26 (1995).

2. See Aurelio Lucchini, *Ideas y formas en la arquitectura nacional* (Montevideo, 1969); Mariano Ariana and Lorenzo Garabelli, *Arquitectura renovadora en Montevideo, 1915–1940. Reflexiones sobre un período fecundo de la arquitectura en el Uruguay* (Montevideo, 1991). For the case of Antonio Bonet, see *Antonio Bonet Castellana* by Fernando Alvarez (Barcelona, 1999); J. F. Liernur, "Antonio Bonet. Some Critical Aspects of His River Plate Works," *Cuadernos del Instituto de Arte Americano* (Buenos Aires, 1995).

3. Among the numerous studies on Torres García, see especially: Miguel A. Battegazzore, *J. Torres Garcia: la trama y los signos* (Montevideo, 1999); Adolfo M. Maslach, *Joaquín Torres-García: sol y luna del arcano* (Caracas, 1998); Mari Carmen Ramírez, ed., *El Taller Torres-García: The School of the South and Its Legacy* (Austin, 1992); Pedro da Cruz, *Torres García and Cercle et Carré: The Creation of Constructive Universalism: Paris 1927–1932* (1994).

4. "The School of the South" was the title of a lecture delivered by Torres García in 1935. During this year he founded, in his own house, the Asociación de Arte Constructivo (AAC).

5. In 1936 Torres García delivered a series of lectures on contemporary painting at the School of Architecture of Universidad de la República.

6. Del Prete took part of the first group Abstraction-Création / Art Non-Figuratif in Paris in 1931. The following year he exhibited his work at the Salon Surindependant in Paris.

7. The name Madí comes from Materialismo Dialectico (Dialectic Materialism). See Gyula Kosice, *Arte Madí* (Buenos Aires, 1982); Mario H. Gradowczyk, *Argentina: Arte Concreto-Invención 1945, Grupo Madí 1946* (New York, 1990).

8. In *Arte Madí Universal* (Buenos Aires) 2 (October 1948).

9. In Tomás Maldonado, *Max Bill* (Buenos Aires, 1955).

10. The manifesto, signed by Berni, Castagnino, Lázaro, Siqueiros, and Spilimbergo, was called *Ejercicio Plástico*. It was published in Buenos Aires in December 1933.

11. H. R. Hitchock, *Latin American Architecture since 1945* (New York, 1955).

12. In fact, Rudofsky was looking for a modern architecture that could overcome the mechanistic determinations that he attributed to a business-oriented profession. For this reason he traveled from Austria to Italy and then to Brazil. He was one of the promoters of the exhibition *Brazil Builds* at the Museum of Modern Art. See B. Rudofsky, "On Architecture and Architects," *New Pencil Points* 4 (April 1943).

13. S. Giedion, *A Decade of New Architecture* (Zurich, 1951).

14. I wish to thank the many Uruguayan friends who helped me gather the information that I used in this article.

15. *Julio Vilamajó: su arquitectura* (Montevideo, 1970); *Facultad de ingeniería* (Montevideo, 1939); César J. Loustau, *Vida y obra de Julio Vilamajó* (Montevideo, 1994); Aurelio Lucchini, *Julio Vilamajó, Su Arquitectura* (Montevideo, 1984).

16. *Mario Payssé-Reyes, 1913–1988* (Montevideo, 1999).

17. Ibid.

18. Ibid.

19. Following the indications of the Second Vatican Council (1962–65), many ideas and practices changed in the Catholic Church. After the Council, a stronger relationship between priests and laics was promoted, especially in Latin America. The existence of an isolated seminary was considered an obstacle to the integration of the seminarists in their community.

20. Quoted in Giangiorgio Pasqualotto, *Avanguardia e tecnologia. Walter Benjamin, Max Bense e i problemi dell'estetica tecnologica* (Rome, 1972).

21. Catalano, quoted in *Eduardo Catalano: Buildings and Projects*, by Camillo Gubitosi and Alberto Izzo (Rome, 1978). Catalano developed this concept in *The Constant: Dialogues on Architecture in Black and White*, by Eduardo Catalano (Cambridge, Mass., 2000). See also Jorge O. Gazaneo and Mabel Scarone, *Eduardo Catalano* (Buenos Aires, 1956).

22. Helio Piñon, *Mario Roberto Alvarez* (Barcelona, 2002).

23. Giulio Carlo Argan, *Walter Gropius e la Bauhaus* (Turin, 1966).

24. Alejandro Crispiani, "Belleza e invención. La estética de lo concreto en los inicios del discurso sobre diseño en la Argentina," in *Block* (Buenos Aires) 1 (August 1997).

25. Janello's work at the University of Buenos Aires was very important. Distinguished figures such as Diana Agrest and Mario Gandelsonas can be mentioned among his disciples. See César Janello, *Texturas* (Buenos Aires, 1961); Lucrecia Escudero Chauvel, "César Janello y las semióticas del espacio," in *Ensayos Semióticos. Dominios, modelos y miradas desde el cruce de la naturaleza y la cultura*, ed. Adrián Gimate-Welsh (Mexico, 2000).

26. See Raúl González Capdevila, *Amancio Williams* (Buenos Aires, 1955); Jorge Silvetti, ed., *Amancio Williams* (New York and Cambridge, Mass., 1987); Amancio Williams, *Amancio Williams* (Buenos Aires, 1990). I sincerely thank Claudio Williams at the Amancio Williams Archive for his help with this research.

27. Delfina Bunge, interview with the author, July 2002.

28. Beatriz Sarlo, *La imaginación técnica* (Buenos Aires, 1992).

29. Amancio Williams, letter to Le Corbusier, January 23, 1946. Amancio Williams Archive.

30. Amancio Williams, letter to Le Corbusier, June 23.,1946. Amancio Williams Archive.

31. Jeffrey Herf, *Reactionary Modernism: Technology, Culture, and Politics in Weimar and the Third Reich* (Cambridge, 1984).

32. Héctor Bernardo, *Para una economía humana* (Buenos Aires, 1949).

33. Ibid. From Bernardo see also: *El régimen corporativo y el mundo actual* (Buenos Aires, 1943). A wonderful analysis of the ideological debates in Argentina during our period is *La Argentina y la tormenta del mundo: idea e ideologías entre 1930 y 1945*, by Tulio Halperin Donghi (Buenos Aires, 2003).

34. See Juan Pablo Bonta, *Eladio Dieste* (Buenos Aires, 1963); Eladio Dieste, *Eladio Dieste: la estructura cerámica* (Bogota, 1987); Eladio Dieste, *Bóvedas arco de directriz catenaria en cerámica armada* (Montevideo, 1985); Remo Pedreschi, *Eladio Dieste* (London, 2000); *Eladio Dieste, 1943–1996* (Sevilla, 1996). See also the astute critical reflection "Dieste: modernità senza conflitti?" by Graciela Silvestri, in *Casabella* 684 (December 2000 / January 2001).

35. Jacques Maritain, *The Responsibility of the Artist* (Princeton, N.J., 1960).

36. Ibid.

37. Pierre Teilhard de Chardin, *The Divine Milieu: An Essay on the Interior Life* (New York, 1968). Quoted in Charles P. Henderson, *God and Science: The Death and Rebirth of Theism* (Louisville, 1986).

38. See *Testamento artístico/Joaquín Torres García* ; estudios críticos, Juan Fló, Eladio Dieste ; Juan Carlos Onetti ; Alvaro Fernández Suárez, Julio E. Payró (Montevideo, 1974).

39. In *Eladio Dieste, 1943–1996* (Sevilla, 1996).

40. Ibid.

THE SEARCH FOR ROOTS IN MEXICAN MODERNISM

JOSÉ ANTONIO
ALDRETE-HAAS

**The history of Mexico, from the Conquest until the
Revolution and beyond, can be regarded as the
search for ourselves, deformed or masked by strange
institutions, and for a Form which expresses us....
We Mexicans have not created a Form which
expresses us. Thus being Mexican cannot be identified
with any form or concrete historical tendency:
it has been an oscillation among several universal
projects translated or imposed and all of them
useless, today. Being Mexican is, then, a reiterated
way of being someone else and living something else.**

OCTAVIO PAZ, *THE LABYRINTH OF SOLITUDE*

Luis Barragán,
Casa Barragán,
Mexico City,
1947–48.

Mexican architecture, from the Revolution of 1910 until the present, can
be interpreted as one continuous search for a form that expresses what
it is to be Mexican. As Paz notes, it is hard to identify any clear historical
tendency in this search: rather, there has been a free swinging between
various local historical references, such as pre-Columbian or colonial,
and several foreign trends that were successively imported and appropriated, or "Mexicanized." This last term is used here to characterize the
attempt to root a foreign style through the use of local materials,
ornament, and murals that make explicit reference to pre-Columbian
and colonial motifs. In other words, there has been a push-and-pull
between the "dis-embedding" forces first of internationalism and now of
globalization (the importation of metropolitan ideas) and the counter-
vailing "re-embedding" forces from the local culture and history—
a natural attempt to feel at home in a modern world. The adoption of
external architectural schemes can be explained by the search for the
techno-scientific ideal of progress, a progress that meant, and still
means, not only enjoying certain material advantages but, above all,

having access to the historical norm and finally becoming "beings of reason." The quest for roots and the Mexicanization of these architectures can be explained by an in-depth internal examination of an identity and a form that fuses tradition with progress.

In this essay, I examine the reception of European avant-garde architecture, with its universal pretensions, in the late 1920s, when Mexico was undergoing a period of accentuated nationalism after the Revolution of 1910. I discuss the terms of its adoption, rather orthodox at first, as well as its increasing Mexicanization during the 1940s and '50s. I identify the causes and the main actors, which I separate into two camps representing two different approaches to the "rooting" of functionalism: one includes architects such as Mario Pani, Juan O'Gorman, and Enrique del Moral, responsible for the design of the National University Campus in the early 1950s. In the other camp, Luis Barragán, with his critical transformation of functionalism, stands alone. This somewhat arbitrary separation is possible only from today's perspective, as it was not until the late 1970s that Barragán received widespread recognition. Moreover, since then his work has been taken, implicitly or explicitly, as the new reference for the idea of roots in architecture, a kind of "new tradition." Thus, an analysis of his work sets the stage for a brief discussion of his legacy and the attitude today toward foreign architecture and the production of Mexican contemporary architecture.

This analysis, which centers on the period between 1939 and 1960, is done from the perspective of a "lonely outsider," to use Paul Feyerabend's romantic expression, since that period is no longer available to us as something we can live. Or, in a way, we can live it only in the mode of pastiche and preference, and that is not really living it since no one lives it with us. What we can do is to make sense of that period from today's perspective, however, is to assess similarities and differences in the way European functionalism was assimilated and transformed at that time and derive implications for the production of architecture today. But first I will begin by reviewing what happened before the 1930s, as a necessary background for the discussion.

Turn-of-the-Century Eclecticism and Postrevolutionary Reactions

A search for roots in Mexican architecture took place just after the armed struggle and before the arrival of the European avant-garde, locally called functionalism. It was a reaction against British and French fin-de-siècle eclecticism; both were considered expressions of modernity during the dictatorship of Porfirio Diaz. It also aimed to heal the

Luis Barragán,
Egerstrom Stables,
State of Mexico,
1967.

Diego Rivera and Juan O'Gorman,
Anahuacalli,
Mexico City,
1935–40.

Juan O'Gorman, Gustavo Saavedra,
and Juan Martinez de Velasco,
Central Library,
National University campus,
Mexico City,
1953.

Rendón Peniche Hospital,
Mérida, Yucatan,
1919.

Juan O'Gorman,
studio for Diego Rivera
and Frida Kahlo,
Mexico City,
1931.

Luis Barragán,
residential building,
Calle Elba, Mexico City,
1939–40.

wounds left by the revolution. The process of reunification demanded a form that would express the ideals of the new unified nation. Two concurrent approaches involved scouring the pre-Columbian past, with doubtful results.[1] One approach, later called national pre-Columbian anachronism, was to incorporate pre-Columbian motifs in colonial architecture. This so-called Mayan Style, launched in the 1920s in Yucatan, incorporated Mayan motifs as decorations on colonial buildings. In the 1930s, pre-Columbian elements were used to "Mexicanize" Art Deco architecture, which had just arrived from Paris and New York; one example was the studio that Diego Rivera built for himself, with the help of architect Juan O'Gorman. Called the Anahuacalli (1935–40), the studio housed Rivera's own work, as well as his extensive collection of pre-Columbian art. These objects were appreciated not only for their archaeological interest but also as pieces with artistic value—a growing trend encouraged by archaeologist Miguel Covarrubias and the newly arrived surrealists, in particular, Wolfgang Paalen.

The other approach was to reevaluate the colonial architectural legacy and to establish a style called neocolonial. The detached *petits châteaux* typologies were abandoned in favor of an architecture with patios, colonial motifs, and traditional materials. This style was thought to capture the "essence" of Mexico since, it was argued, colonial architecture already blended pre-Hispanic and Spanish influences. It was adopted as the official stance during the 1920s and '30s, in particular for symbolic public buildings such as administration buildings and schools. It was perceived, more than the other, as the new face for the postrevolutionary governments. This approach was eventually deformed into a domestic fashion that sought to copy, in new urban developments like one called Chapultepec Heights, the Californian style popular in that state at the time.

It was in the context of this architectural production, during the late 1920s, when the political and economic reconstruction of the country was under way, that functionalism made its appearance in Mexico. It was accepted with not a little antagonism from the other camps; the argument was made that the colonial style, with its massiveness, small openings, and plan limitations, was unsuitable for specific functional buildings such as schools, hospitals, and public housing, which were important elements in the construction of the new state.[2] The functionalists adopted as their point of departure the European trust in function and technical innovation. The materials included concrete, already in use for some twenty years, some glass and iron, and also brick. The results, which vary in terms of quality, were perceived as being not only modern, but also Mexican. Modern because they provided an answer to newly defined postrevolutionary social concerns such as housing, health, and education, with programs, architecture, and technology that essentially differed little from their European counterparts. There was the widespread adoption of the functionalist formal language, including Le Corbusier's pilotis, roof terraces, and *brises-soleil* built in exposed concrete. And Mexican because they responded to local problems and were built with locally available technology and materials. One of the first works to illustrate the new style was Juan O'Gorman's studio for Diego Rivera and Frida Kahlo, built in 1930, and his 1934 design for the building of the newly constituted National Confederation of Workers. Other examples are the National Institute of Cardiology, built in 1937 by José Villagrán García, considered the ideologue of functionalism in Mexico, and the National Music Conservatory, built in 1946 by Mario Pani. Private developers adopted the same architectural discourse because it provided an image of modernity. Examples include several office and apartment buildings from the 1930s and '40s by Del Moral, Pani, and Luis Barragán, who was in his modernist period.

The "Mexicanization" of International Architecture

By the late 1940s, postrevolutionary reconstruction was complete and the country's economic development was in full gear, due in part to the implementation of the Alianza para el Progreso (a sort of Marshall Plan for Latin America), which increased the influx of foreign capital into the country: roads and irrigation infrastructure were built, as well as housing, hospitals, and schools. Mexico required a new face that would express its access to postwar economic expansion, to modernity, but this face needed to be "Mexican." Hence, the effort to culturally "re-embed" architecture, in particular that built by the government: the more orthodox adoption of the International Style gave way to some efforts to "Mexicanize" it.

One of the major works of the period was the campus of the National University in Mexico City. According to some critics of the time, it represents a victory over "historical anachronisms" by an architecture that synthesizes the modern qualities of functionalism with a nationalistic architecture.[3] The mere size of the enterprise had no precedent, nor did the diversity of positions represented by the designs. Three different versions of functionalism were expressed, all derived from the European ideology, as interpreted by José Villagrán García, who was also the teacher of several of the participating architects. The first version was formulated by those close to the orthodoxy of their mentor, who himself adhered to the strict credo advocated by Juan O'Gorman and Juan Legorreta in their work of the early 1930s. Representative examples of this type of functionalism can be found in buildings such as the School of Science, by Raul Cacho and Felix Sanchez, and the

Engineering School. The second group of functionalists, accused of being formalist by the first camp, included Pani, who had studied at the Ecole des Beaux-Arts in Paris and headed the overall project together with Enrique del Moral. Their architecture was accused of being "more elastic," "less ascetic," and "less austere." They were responsible for the design of the Administration building. And the third group included individuals whose designs were unique in that they integrated pre-Columbian references into modernism. Examples of their work are the Central Library by Juan O'Gorman, the stadium by Augusto Perez Palacios, and the *Frontones* (Fronton Courts) by Alberto Arai.

In all cases, three main strategies were employed to "Mexicanize" the International Style: (1) the profuse use of local materials (in this case, volcanic rock found on-site), on walls and pavement; (2) the incorporation of formal references from the pre-Columbian past, such as large plazas, taluds in the stadium, and the *frontones*; (3) the incorporation of murals in buildings regarded as symbolic, such as the Main Administration building, the School of Science, the School of Medicine, and the library, among others. This last gesture was not new: muralist José Clemente Orozco had already collaborated with Pani on a building for the Teachers' Association and on a large housing complex, as had the Guatemalan painter Carlos Merida. Such partnerships accentuated the link between architecture and the prestigious muralist movement, regarded as a paramount expression of postrevolutionary art. From then on, the incorporation of murals into architecture proliferated and amounted to what was later regarded as *Integración Plástica* (Plastic Integration),[4] which also included the incorporation of figurative sculptures in plazas and lobbies and the design of *brises-soleil* and other elements by artists, as seen in the Anthropology Museum, built by Pedro Ramírez Vázquez in the early 1960s.

Barragán: A Critical Path

In the context of such a varied production of architecture, the work of Luis Barragán, called "the Mexican Other" by one critic,[5] was regarded not as "true architecture" but as "scenery." In 1951 Villagrán summarized his view on Barragán, as well as his own position and consequently that of the functionalists:

The architecture of our good friend Barragán has a decorative value. It has a high value, though its basic intention is not completely contemporary. In other words, it disintegrates the architectonic, which explains why, when plastic artists (and not architects) evaluate his work, they recognize it as being highly artistic and do not understand why it is considered not completely architectonic. They should bear in mind that architecture is impure art, that among its values are the useful, hierarchically inferior to the aesthetic, and the social, which is superior, and that when someone sacrifices one or the other or both of those values partially or totally, the work's plastic value is that of scenery or decoration and not authentic architecture.[6]

Today, however, Barragán's work sheds a new critical light on the work of most of his contemporaries: it shows a timid revision of early modernist propositions, not beyond the superficial incorporation of local references and materials.[7] "His art is modern but not modernist, is universal but not an image of New York or Milan," said Paz after Barragán was granted the Pritzker Prize in 1980.[8]

His mature work, from the early 1940s to the late 1970s, manifests a critical attitude toward both positions, European functionalism and its Mexicanization. He appears as a "light in the labyrinth" of imitations and anachronisms. His inspiration came not only from colonial architecture and pre-Columbian temples, but also from indigenous constructions of Mexican pueblos, North African Casbahs, and the architecture of southern Spain. He saw Mexico not in nationalistic terms as a geographic entity but as part of a larger culture encompassing Spain, North Africa, and parts of the Middle East; he drew references from these areas, incorporating them into his work, transforming European functionalism.

Barragán turned away from internationalism *per se* and moved toward considering the International Style as a tradition of principles and forms to be appropriated and changed according to local needs. He modified the modernist notion of transparency to respond to the bright light of sunny Mexico and to the traditional need for privacy of the Mexican and Mediterranean dwelling. He used a narrow, low-ceilinged, dark entrance corridor derived from the Mediterranean *zaguan* to make the transition between the intense light and public character of the street and the intimacy and half light of the internal spaces. The size of windows is not always large but qualified in order to create dark, intimate corners, bring the garden into the interior, or direct the view toward a tree, a fountain, or the sky. Barragán transformed Le Corbusier's roof gardens into dreamlike closed patios, with only a window to the sky. He questioned technology by revaluing the traditional wall, giving greater scale and massiveness to the pure and flattened volumes of modernism. And he provided this wall with a skin of color, of popular origins, so as "to reduce or enlarge space or to provide [it] with a magical touch and to produce joy," to use his own words.[9] In so doing, he "re-embedded" international architecture by firmly anchoring his work to his cultural locality and landscape and opening the possibility for the use of color elsewhere.

Like some of his contemporaries in Europe, such as Team X, Barragán reacted against the rigid rationality of the early modernists

Mario Pani,
National Conservatory
of Music,
Mexico City,
1946.

Mario Pani, Enrique del Moral,
and Salvador Ortega Flores,
Administration Building,
National University, Mexico City,
1953.

Roberto Alvarez Espinoza, Pedro Ramirez
Vasquez, and Ramon Torres,
School of Medicine,
National University, Mexico City,
1953.

Augusto Perez Palacios, Raúl Salinas Moro,
and Jorge Bravo Jiménez,
Stadium,
National University, Mexico City,
1963.

Luis Barragán,
Casa Barragán,
Mexico City,
1947–48.
Living-room window.

Luis Barragán,
Casa Barragán,
1947–48.
Roof patio.

Luis Barragán,
El Bebedero, Las Arboledas,
State of Mexico,
1960.

and humanized architecture by reinforcing its relationship to nature and the patterns of ordinary life. For him, architecture had to go beyond function in order to create emotions like serenity, intimacy, and surprise as an antidote to the dehumanization of functionalist architecture. Space is perceived in its totality but not fully discovered because the open floor plans are interrupted by low screens that create corners with a sense of enclosure and intimacy. Circulation spaces are not based on a strict economic program, but rather designed so as to enhance the architectural experience with an element of surprise. And nature is celebrated by handling water, plants, and animals such as horses as architectural elements. For Barragán, landscape was architecture without a roof and constituted a single continuous space with architecture. No different from his architecture, gardens were to elicit surprise, to enchant, and to create an atmosphere for "spontaneous meditation." Gardens were to be *places*, not simply pieces of visual decoration. And they were not inspired by the modernist gardens of the time but by memories of those he had experienced when horseback riding in his youth, in the hill of Jalisco.

Finally, unlike the examples of Integración Plástica, Barragán's integration of landscape—nature, water, land—and architecture, the built and the unbuilt, light and color, lies between the surrealism of De Chirico and some of the work of early 1960s minimalist artists like Richard Serra, Dan Flavin, and others, thus confirming Barragán's deep phenomenological position, in contrast to those who were guided by the orthodoxy of the architectural credo of the time. His work was influenced by his distance from the self-referential debate of the profession and by his association with friends such as the naïve-art painter Jesus "Chucho" Reyes, who opened his eyes to Mexican folk art, in particular its use of color; muralist José Clemente Orozco, who affirmed his tendency toward a formal synthesis that favors the abstract side of *lo mexicano* with paintings such as *Pueblo Mexicano*; and sculptor Mathias Goeritz, who shared his formal sensibility and his knowledge of European avant-garde art, particularly in projects such as the Satellite Towers (1957–58) and the Tlalpan Chapel (1951–54).

Mexican Architecture Today

Today, Mexican architects still debate how to be modern while at the same time returning to the idea of origin, but in a way that is different from Barragán's approach and usually without his critical attitude. The idea of origin, formerly associated with colonial or pre-Colombian references, gave way, in Barragán's work, to unique solutions. His architecture became the new referent, directly or indirectly; it acquired the status of a "new tradition." It is a tradition that sometimes inspires works of quality, although in most cases the new work embodies empty expressions of his formal language, devoid of emotional content. It is, however, a fashion that is attractive for local consumption and even for export. But also has generated opposition: some think this "new tradition" must be rejected for the sake of "modernity"—identified now, as in bygone eras, with the architectonic production of the economic metropolis. Thus copies of architecture produced in the United States, Japan, or Europe are uncritically considered examples of modernity. These are also successful products for local consumption, but less so for export.

Among those who have followed this new tradition is Ricardo Legorreta, who was the first to skillfully refer to Barragán's formal vocabulary while developing a language of his own and applying it not only to residences but also to banks, office buildings, hotels, and even factories. Others have followed Legorreta's use of scale and color with doubtful results. And others have made nostalgic reference to his early work in Guadalajara or use his walls, forms, and color in an eclectic blend with somewhat pseudocontemporary elements.

High-tech and, more recently, minimalist architecture and its variations, with a profusion of steel and glass, are seen as expressions of modernity to be emulated. They embrace again, as in the 1940s and '50s, and in spite of repeated criticisms, the techno-scientific program, with its notions of efficiency and universality. As in the time of early modernism, it is taken as axiomatic that social and economic development derives from the wise use of technology. These theories enjoyed fertile ground in the late 1980s and ever since. They provide images to accompany Mexico's dream of becoming part of the First World—the result of a commercial treaty with U.S. and Canada (NAFTA). This dream became a nightmare when, in December 1994, Mexico entered an acute political and economic crisis resulting from massive capital outflow, a crisis that has been painful to leave behind.[10] But in Mexico it was not everyday reality, characterized by dramatic inequalities in personal incomes, that called this premise into question; however, the execution of these "modern" buildings has proved to be the result of handicraft technology more than the work of specialized, white-robed technicians. Even so, the growing forces of globalization and the permanent illusion of "being modern" keep the market for such structures alive.

This simplified overview of contemporary Mexican architecture does not end here.[11] Not only are there those who adhere to the new tradition and those who oppose it, but there also exists an architecture that appears to recognize Barragán's teachings in terms of his critical attitude toward his own culture as well as toward external influences, a criticism that can only come from one's own roots. Clearly

Luis Barragán,
Las Capuchinas chapel,
Mexico City,
1953–60.

Luis Vicente Flores,
School of Dance,
National Center for the Arts,
Mexico City,
1994.

this architecture does not necessarily resort to his unique formal language. In other words, it seeks to go beyond naïve "nationalisms" or "folkloric reductionism" or the simple adoption of international formulas. It is also an architecture that shows a critical attitude toward the values of today's global society, which Gilles Lipovetsky has called "the Void Era,"[12] values that are not so different from those of Barragán's time: the indiscriminate fascination with technology, the loss of privacy, the emphasis on image rather than content, and the instrumental view of nature that has almost brought about the destruction of the planet. Furthermore, this architecture draws on strategies that are still valid: to assert that technology is a simple tool, manifest as much in the ancient cutting of stone as in the use of huge panels of glass; to subordinate technology to the creation of emotions such as serenity, intimacy, and surprise, among others, as antidotes to today's emphasis on consumption; to adopt the phenomenological vision of architecture[13] in opposition to those who give preference to formal and technological pirouettes justified by obscure pseudophilosophical constructs offering very little emotional gratification; to seek a sensory experience in which color, sound, form, texture, and temperature are part of a totality, in open opposition to the "decorated shed" promoted by a society addicted to the spectacle that has now become virtual; and to use the wealth of nature, transforming the rain, sunsets, and vegetation into architectonic elements, restoring to nature her primordial role in architecture.

In sum, our analysis as "lonely outsiders" of modernism in Mexico shows that some elements remain constant after half a century in spite of the changing circumstances. Mexican contemporary architecture still searches for a form that expresses what is to be Mexican. However, it is a form suitable for a Mexico that no longer meets the romantic view portrayed by Sergei Eisenstein's *Qué Viva Mexico* or the violent and socially conscious perspective of the Muralists, but that of a society, like many others, struggling to belong to the Global Village without losing its identity. For some, this form should maintain and enhance the new tradition established by the formal language of Barragán, while for others that form should be no different from what is regarded as the "new internationalism": the architecture produced in Switzerland, Holland, Japan, or the U.S., which paradoxically, on closer scrutiny, appears rather local. Still for others, that form should result not from the easy import of foreign formulas or from the nostalgic replication of the new tradition but from a critical appraisal of the local and the global, as done by Alvaro Siza, Tadao Ando, and Peter Zumthor, among others. And only time will tell if there is another "Mexican other" capable of a similar creative cultural exchange and synthesis so much needed in today's world.

Notes

1. For an analysis of these styles, see Ernesto Alva Martinez "La Búsqueda de una Identidad," in *La Arquitectura Mexicana del Siglo XX* by Gonzalez Gortazar (Mexico City: Consejo Nacional para La Cultura y Las Artes, 1994), 36–53. See also Enrique X. de Anda Alanis, *La Arquitectura de la Revolución Mexicana: Corrientes y estilos en la década de los veintes* (Mexico City: Universidad Nacional Autónoma de México, 1990).

2. See Israel Katzmann, *La Arquitectura Contemporánea Mexicana*, precedentes y desarrollo (Mexico City: Instituto Nacional de Antropología e Historia, 1964), and Salvador Pinocelly, "La Arquitectura en México 1940–1960," in *Apuntes para la historia y crítica de la arquitectura mexicana del siglo XX: 1900–1980* (Mexico City: Instituto Nacional de Bellas Artes, 1982).

3. See Jorge Alberto Manrique, "El Futuro Radiante de la Ciudad," in *La Arquitectura Mexicana del Siglo XX*, 125–47.

4. See Alberto Hijar, "La Integración Plástica," in *La Arquitectura Mexicana*, 148–53.

5. Kenneth Frampton, *The Mexican Other* (Japan: Yutaka Saito, Toto Shuppan), 1992.

6. See "Carta a un amigo," August 2, 1951, in *Documentos para la historia de la arquitectura en México* by Ramón Vargas Salguero and José Villagrán (Mexico City: Instituto Nacional de Bellas Artes, 1986), 288–90.

7. For a more in-depth discussion of the contribution of Barragán's work to Mexican architecture, see José Antonio Aldrete-Haas, *El Legado de Luis Barragán y La Renovación de la Cultura* in ANALES del Instituto de Investigaciones Estéticas, UNAM, 1995), 69–95, and "Light in the Labyrinth, or the Teachings of Luis Barragan," in *The Quiet Revolution*, ed. Federica Zanco (Milan: Skira, 2001), 274–83.

8. Octavio Paz, "Luis Barragan y los usos de la tradición," in *Los Privilegios de la Vista* (Mexico City: Fondo de Cultura Económoca, 1987), 186–88.

9. See Mario Schetnan, *El Arte de hacer Arquitectura o como hacer Arte: Entrevista con Luis Barragán* (Mexico: Revista Entorno, vol. 1, Year 1, January 1982).

10. As a result of the massive flight of capital, there was political uncertainty generated by the guerrilla uprising in Chiapas and the political assassination of the presidential candidate of the ruling party.

11. Architectural production in Mexico is more complex and includes other actors, such as Teodoro González de León, Abraham Zabludovsky, Carlos Mijares, and finally Agustin Hernandez, whose work is well known in Mexico.

12. Gilles Lipovetsky, *L'ère du vide. Essais sur l'individualisme contemporain* (Paris: Edition Gallimrd, 1983).

13. See José Antonio Aldrete-Haas, *La Habitacion de la Memoria: La Casa de Luis Barragán en Tacubaya, México* (Milan: Lotus International, December 2003).

ANTILLEAN ARCHITECTURE OF THE FIRST MODERNITY: 1930–1945

The Theoretical Foundations of Tropical Rationalism

Guillermo González
Sánchez,
Copello Building,
Santo Domingo,
1939.
Interior view of stair with
glass-brick wall.

Theoretical texts did not accompany the assimilation of European rationalist formal and spatial codes in the Caribbean, as they did in Mexico, Brazil, and Argentina. With the exception of a few academics, professionals lacked the opportunities and motivation for writing and instead focused on project- and construction-based work. Given the lack of specialized magazines in the Antilles, there were few outlets for the diffusion of ideas. In Havana, the regular publication of *Arquitectura* was the exception; in its pages a small group of local architects would appear repeatedly. To a certain extent, professional associations helped fill this void. In 1933 the Puerto Rico Institute of Architects was created, as were the only schools of architecture in the region, in Havana and Santo Domingo. In both, the principles of the modern movement were taught by young professionals who had been trained abroad—from the Dominican Republic, Leo Pou Ricart (Belgium), José Antonio Caro (France), Guillermo González (United States)—or by the generation of students who rebelled against Beaux-Arts training. In 1947, for instance, the students at the Havana Faculty of Architecture, in a violent gesture of rejection, burned books by famed Renaissance architect Giacomo Vignola.[1]

In these decades, personal contact with famous international architects was limited, since the visits of the masters were brief. In 1939 José Lluis Sert stopped in Havana on his way to the United States; in 1945 Richard J. Neutra visited Santo Domingo and Havana and worked in San Juan de Puerto Rico; in 1949 Walter Gropius lectured in Cuba.[2] This explains the fragile bond with the European experience and the more significant weight carried by North American "modernity." It is not by accident that in 1932 the General Assembly of the Architects Union of Havana opted to appoint Frank Lloyd Wright an honorary member. The medium for this cultural transmission of architectural ideas was magazines and the few books that did not distinguish between conceptual paradigms and the application of isolated formal elements. This is evident in the two main theoretical texts, one by Alberto Camacho[3] and the other by Joaquín E. Weiss,[4] that publicized the new international tendencies in Cuba. In them, the figure of Le Corbusier dominated through the strength of his writings (but not the built projects), which appeared alongside the work of André Lurçat, Robert Mallet-Stevens, Auguste Perret, Djo Bourgeois, Michel Roux-Spitz, and Gabriel Guevrekian. At the same time, the skyscraper was the most innovative expression, technically and formally, and it was given extensive coverage.[5]

Alberto Camacho referred to rationalism in terms of reinforced concrete and identified Le Corbusier and Pierre Jeanneret as "extremist" architects, and Joaquín Weiss characterized the movement as "radical" and "elementalist." Thus we find a certain resistance, among most professionals from the Caribbean, to the social, functional, and technological program of the European avant-garde. This feeling arose from the fact that many architects, still immersed in the academic tradition, identified with neocolonialism, under the influence of Latin American theoreticians such as Angel Guido[6] and the American Nathaniel C. Curtis. The latter, in a lecture at Havana University, developed a biting critique of the Swiss pavilion and of the inherent primitivism in the *pilotis*.[7] Still, the technical and environmental problems were separate from the new aesthetic values: in those years, colonial traditions in climate control (the use of the *brise-soleil*, for example) were more important than the studies of Alexander Klein, Ernst Neufert, Gropius, or Le Corbusier on the functional and thermal efficiency of the house.[8] Once again, the role of the avant-garde was closer to the sphere of plastic and literary artists. Alejo Carpentier, for one, immediately grasped the innovative content of "live architecture" and of Le Corbusier's "machine for living," identifying it closely with the work of Picasso, Stravinsky, Cocteau, Varèse, De Chirico, and the Cuban painter Marcelo Pogolotti.[9]

In the 1940s, this situation changed, following José Lluis Sert's brief contact with the local architects in 1939[10] and the presence in Havana of Martín Domínguez, a Barcelonian member of the Grupo de Artistas y Técnicos Españoles para el Progreso de la Arquitectura Contemporánea (GATEPAC). They inspired the creation of Cuban affiliates to CIAM, led by Eugenio Batista, and the formation in 1941 of the ATEC group (Technical Grouping of Contemporary Studies), which brought together professionals of the so-called fifties' generation: Miguel Gastón, Nicolás Arroyo, Beatriz Menéndez, Beatriz Masó, Emilio del Junco, Eduardo Montoulieu, Manuel de Tapia Ruano, and others. At the same time, Pedro Martínez Inclán headed the Pro-Urbanism Patronage (1942), which addressed issues of city planning. Very soon, a bond grew between local traditions and the principles of CIAM, as is evident in a statement from the Pro-Urbanism Patronage: "Architecture is the technique of building that makes use of the most appropriate methods and materials for the task, according to the character, site, and economic conditions, to define a space functionally appropriate to the objective and in this way, achieves a space and form expressive of artistic, scientific and industrial 'zeitgeist' of the country in which the work has been conceived and executed."[11]

In the first meeting of this group in the historical colonial city of Trinidad, the necessity of preserving the historical heritage was affirmed, but the members also participated in the international architectural debate: in 1947, Eugenio Batista and Nicolás Arroyo attended the sixth CIAM in Bridgewater, England. A Cuban delegation, comprised of Joaquín E. Weiss, Pedro Martínez Inclán, and the young Antonio Quintana, attended the sixth Pan-American Congress of Architects in Lima in 1947. This is important because of the definition of "contemporary architecture" as an expression of the regional situation; the works of Rafael de Cárdenas, Alberto Prieto, Aquiles Capablanca, and Antonio Santana received awards in that event, and the theoretical exchange of ideas among colleagues throughout the continent began.

The Architectural Avant-Garde

Several theories have been put forward regarding the transmission of European rationalist codes in Latin America.[12] The Spanish critic Eduardo Subirats described the adaptation of the language of "white boxes"—in Brazil it was called anthropophagy—as transforming the object from the context of its origin.[13] This practice occurred on the islands, where the culture is not purely western but is more a product of the mix of Asian, African, and European immigrants with the native Amerindians, resulting in a syncretic culture that diverged from the Cartesian rationalism

Richard Neutra,
open classrooms for the schools of Puerto Rico,
1944.

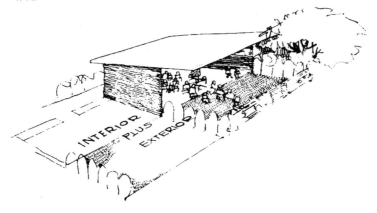

Richard Neutra,
project for the 600-bed district hospital,
Puerto Rico,
1944.

Pedro Martínez Inclán,
Justo Carrillo apartment building,
Havana,
1944.

that was prevalent in the 1920s. Here, the true assimilation of the modern movement started in 1945, when the first examples of works by the Brazilian, Mexican, and Venezuelan avant-garde became known, along with the work of architects who immigrated to the United States to escape the Nazis: Gropius, Sert, Breuer, Neutra, Mies, Albers, Moholy-Nagy, and others.

From the 1930s on, there was a scattered appropriation of the rationalist vocabulary, owing to the following factors: (a) the propagation of reinforced concrete as the "modern" construction material; (b) the greater diversity of social functions and their expression at an urban scale; (c) the growing presence of commercial buildings realized by developers, technicians, and engineers, who abandoned cultural content and symbolical attributes; (d) the disappearance of the Beaux-Arts language restrictions and the integration of formal codes, dissimilar but equivalent, in the identification of modernity: rationalism, modern monumental, and Art Deco; (e) the use of "fragments" from the formal repertoire as aesthetic characterization—windows, balconies, plinths, and cornices; (f) the North American version of the European language in the official buildings of the New Deal—Depression Modern and the Streamline Modern;[14] (g) the influence of Hollywood sets as representations of contemporary life.[15]

Of the professionals who adhered to these principles, few were able to meld the external influences and the internal factors into a coherent language. On most of the islands, the academic tradition still prevailed in the reiteration of vernacular elements or the acceptance of the neocolonial Art Deco. In Haiti, the Victorian gingerbread style was replaced by a regionalism transplanted from the south of France, as is evident in the houses in Pétionville designed by Max Ewald and Robert Baussan.[16] In Puerto Rico, local resistance to innovations—perhaps a refusal to identify directly with the United States—can be seen in the work of Pedro A. De Castro, Joseph J. O'Kelly, Fidel Sevillano, Santiago Iglesias, and Pedro Méndez Mercado. Richard J. Neutra visited the island in 1943, having been invited by Rexford G. Tugwell, then governor of Puerto Rico, to oversee plans for hospitals and public schools.[17] This opened the way to a conceptual assimilation of the modern movement, not in formal terms but in the methodology of design: an adjustment to the climatic conditions of the tropics and the use of construction techniques suited to the economic situation in developing countries.[18] In spite of Neutra's influence on the repertoire of luxurious houses for the Caribbean bourgeoisie, the more significant legacy is the elaboration of a contemporary language that was neither anonymous nor schematic but rather based on local social and economical factors. This contemporary language marked the research of young architects in the 1950s.[19]

The Dominican Guillermo González Sánchez (1900–70) and the Cuban Eugenio Batista y González de Mendoza (1900–91) constitute the Antillean paradigms for this period: both were born at the beginning of the century, graduated in the same decade, produced their first significant work in 1939, and followed different paths but identified with the postulates of the modern movement. Both navigated a similar parabola, achieving a moment of splendor in the 1940s, then declining in the 1950s. They are the masters responsible for the aesthetic and conceptual formation of the local avant-garde, but these new ideas were not expressed in their own work, which was more conservative.

Guillermo González spearheaded the movement to revamp Dominican architecture and design education; he was followed by José Antonio Caro, Humberto Ruiz Castillo, and the engineer Ramón Báez López Penha. González began his studies at Columbia University in New York and graduated from Yale in 1930, having designed a Beaux-Arts project, the Municipal Palace of Santo Domingo, which was influenced by the romantic Swedish nationalism of Ragnar Ostberg. His eight-month stay in Europe put him in contact with the masters—he visited Mies's pavilion in Barcelona, and he identified with the avant-gardists who came of age in those years. After working with Edward D. Stone and Francis Keally in the United States, he returned to Santo Domingo to concentrate on his career. In 1939 he built the Copello office building on Duarte Street, one of the main streets of the historical center of the Dominican capital. Representative of the rationalist ortho-doxy, it has continuous bands of parapets and windows, reflecting the influence of Oud and Mendelsohn. Quoting Le Corbusier and Pierre Chareau, the stairs are identified by a vertical brick-and-glass area that illuminates a slender reinforced-concrete structure. Are there any local elements in the work? In contrast to the previous tall eclectic buildings, there is a desire to respect the scale of the traditional architecture, to conserve the base in relation to the street and upper volume, and to modulate the light in the public areas. The reaffirmation of a progressive modern image implied an aesthetic as well as an ideological stance against the predominant classical monumentalist language of the Trujillo era.

During the dictatorship of Leónidas Trujillo, who governed the Dominican Republic from 1930 to 1961, advanced modern archi-tecture, which was to be financed by the government and to project an image of freedom, internationalism, and progress, received only ambiva-lent and inconsistent support. We find the use of contradictory codes and the expression of a double standard, characteristic of authoritarian political systems. Two hotels constructed during Trujillo's reign, the Jaragua in Santo Domingo (1941, demolished in 1985), and the Hamaca in Boca Chica (1951), reveal a desire to "tropicalize" the International

Style. The Jaragua reflects the modernization of the country's infra- structure. Designed with an eye to international—mainly North American—tourism, it was built during the difficult times of World War II, without the necessary construction materials. González viewed architec- ture as a neutral system mediating between function and landscape. In dialogue with the Santo Domingo sea wall and the vertical row of palms that frame the views toward the blue sea, he placed a white volume whose simplicity, order, rhythm, and composition juxtapose the precision of the rational object with the natural environment. This is assimilated, not through the immediacy of a pure geometry/free nature nexus, but rather through a succession of cinematic perceptions, akin to Renaissance perspective models, that are generated by the shaded social spaces on the Jaragua's ground floor. Thus the spaces are inte- grated into the landscape while assimilating in their interior the tropical vegetation, or as it occurs in the Hamaca, the sea water that bathes the pilotis of the main volume.

In its time the Jaragua hotel was the social center of the Dominican bourgeoisie. The hotel became the first Caribbean example of a coherent application of the modern movement's codes, and it implied the abandonment of the neocolonial folklorism that had spread on the islands and also the Art Deco exoticism of the Puerto Rican Hotel Normandie. Gradually this type of architecture was accepted and applied in public buildings and some private residences, such as Guillermo González's Jaraguita apartments (1945) and his Pichardo House (1947) in the Gazcue neighborhood. Here, the volumetric articu- lation of the previous work is further opened to the landscape through the use of shaded galleries, large glass surfaces, and long, continuous balconies. In the following decade, this would lead to the mature work of the Peace and Confraternity Fair of the Free World (1955).

Eugenio Batista, who also received an academic Beaux- Arts education, was more interested in the search for local cultural attributes. He graduated from Havana University in 1924,[20] and he worked in the studio of Leonardo Morales at a time when the neo- colonial language prevailed. Batista collaborated with the Havana Plan team led by J. L. N. Forestier, integrating the Port Amphitheater (1934) within its scheme—an example of the fusion between a classical composition and the naturalism of the local Havana limestone. Batista traveled to Europe and the United States and found himself more attracted to the works of Asplund and Greene & Greene than he was to Le Corbusier's machine aesthetic. In the 1930s he participated in the movement to restore colonial Cuban architecture and refurbish older structures as housing for the middle and upper classes. This work was published in *Social* and *Grafos* magazines. Other designers and architects from Havana who took part in this movement include

Clara Porcet, Enrique Luis Varela, Víctor Morales, Manuel de Tapia Ruano, and Silvio Acosta.

What distinguished Batista from his contemporaries was his capacity to distance himself from the colonial decorative and compositional system and his ability to synthesize the conceptual foundations of this colonial heritage. He established the "system of the three Ps"—patios, portals, persians—as the characteristic elements of the Cuban house that were suited to the local way of life and to the climate.[21] This is evident in the residences for Eutimio Falla Bonet (1938), Jorge Hernández Trelles (1939), Alina Johnson (1941), María Teresa Aróstegui (1941), and the one for himself (1943), all in Havana. The Alberto Kaffenburg mansion by Rafael de Cárdenas (awarded the 1940 Gold Medal by the College of Architects) is a design that mixed Cuban colonial elements with the typical attributes of Californian or Floridean architecture. Batista's solution is original in plan and in the accomplished synthesis of the use of whitewashed brick, clay tile roofs, wood galleries, continuous windows facing the sea, and light transparency of the covered terrace around the pool, all representative elements of the rationalist formal codes. This architecture expresses the contrast between two cultures: the old ascetic mansions of the traditional aristocracy and the ostentatious status symbols of the new merchant class.

In his personal residence, the organization of the floor plan reflects the functional differentiation of spaces and an asymmetrical composition that is identified with a Nordic neo-empirism (i.e., Asplund). The patio is fragmented to achieve the introversion of living spaces, and the terraces and galleries adopt the modulation and lightness of colonial arcades but with the virtual filter of wooden grids, a reference to the modulation of Japanese tatamis. The result is a Cuban house that reflects a universal aesthetic. It is a pity that his public work did not advance along the same path. In the Payret Theater (1951) in Havana, he fell back on academic historicism. In the Trust Company of Cuba bank in the Miramar neighborhood (1955), he applied an abstract monumentalism. Nevertheless, his writing and teaching at the school of architecture of the Catholic University of Villanueva were valuable.

In the 1940s the expansion of the urban middle class and the availability of resources facilitated the construction of rental apartments and single-family houses in the suburbs. The abstract language of pure forms, as well as the economic advantages in the construction process, was seen as a demonstration of modernity and confidence in the future. Technological advancement was also highly valued in the postwar period as an expression of the American way of life. In the center of Havana we find a Mendelsohnian expressionism in the balconies of the Solimar apartments (1945) by Manuel Copado; the aesthetic restraint of Alberto Prieto's language in the first collective

Guillermo González Sánchez,
Pichardo House,
Santo Domingo,
1944.

Guillermo González Sánchez,
Copello Building,
Santo Domingo,
1944.

Manuel Copado,
Solimar apartment building,
Havana,
1944.

Eugenio Batista,
Eutimio Falla Bonet Residence,
Havana,
1938.
View of the swimming pool by the sea.

Max Borges Recio,
Santiago Claret Residence,
Havana,
1941.

Rafael de Cárdenas,
Miramar clinic,
Havana,
1940–50.

Nicolás Arroyo and
Gabriela Menéndez,
Berta Garcia apartment building,
Havana,
1944.

housing buildings; a persistence of the *cortijo* in the planimetry of the Santeiro building (1937) by Emilio de Soto; a difficult eclectic balance between the colonial, organic, and functionalist repertoire in Gustavo Botet's residences; a cubist volumetric composition in the apartments by the Almendares River by Rafael de Cárdenas, and a pivoting dynamism of the vertical circulation in Miramar apartments by Emilio de Junco, Miguel Gastón, and Martín Domínguez.[22]

The theme of the single-family house in Cuba reflects the assimilation of two creatively reelaborated paradigms: first, the Wrightian vocabulary in Gabriela Menéndez and Nicolás Arroyo's own house (1917) in El Reparto Miramar (1943); second, the Gropius and Breuer vocabulary in the house in the Malecón (sea wall) by Max Enrique Borges (1918) and the Country Club's Noval House (1951) by Mario Romañach. Romañach was trained in Eugenio Batista's school and traveled the slow road from the stereotyped models of Californian colonial to the mature mastery of the modern movement, becoming the most distinguished designer of the 1950s generation.

The Noval House has not lost its poetic message or its original freshness. The free decomposition of orthodox vocabulary, the interrelation of functional volumes and natural surrounding space, the transparency and continuity of the circulation system, the presence of vegetation in the transparent spaces of the house, all position it more precisely within the neorationalist quest of the 1980s *white* (Richard Meier) rather than in the orthodox functionalist purism. It marks the beginning of a new phase in the evolution of Cuban architecture as it moved toward an original identity.[23]

Building Policies of the Benefactor State

In the Caribbean, the 1930s and '40s were characterized by State initiatives in the construction of social works and the application of the principles of the modern movement. Although most of these initiatives did not coincide with the formal and spatial paradigms of the avant-garde, they nevertheless revealed a repertoire on an urban and rural scale that allowed for a change in the predominant aesthetic values, which were still conditioned by academicism. A certain kinship remained between the "design" architecture and the works built by government planners, and despite the latter group's functionalist schematism, they maintained a high technical-functional standard and good construction quality. The tendency to value the homogeneity of a system of functions was apparent in the sixth Pan-American Congress of Architects in Lima, where the Public Works Ministry of Cuba and the Schools, Hospitals and Urbanism Project Offices received awards. The foreign models were adopted from three main sources: the social works from the 1930s in Europe (Germany, Holland, France); the symbolic and monumental examples of authoritarian states (Germany, France, Italy, and Spain); the massive construction carried out during Roosevelt's New Deal through federal agencies that offered the unemployed manual labor and the opportunity to create an infrastructure of national services: the Works Progress Administration, the United States Housing Authority, and the Farm Security Administration.[24]

On the English and French islands of the Caribbean, the prewar "modern monumental" prevailed, still under the influence of the repertoire set forth in the 1937 Paris International Exhibition. In the 1940s, government buildings, post offices, and hospitals were built using a common language based on simple white volumes with cylindrical columned porches to indicate the main entrance. These have greater formal looseness, as in the Hôpital-Hospice, designed by Ali Tur in Point-à-Pitre, Guadeloupe, and the Syndicates' House in Fort de France, Martinique. The latter, with its circular plan, has a strong coherence in the handling of the functionalist codes, as well as an interior patio, which was essential in the Caribbean climate.

At this time, Puerto Rico had more advanced expressions of the Antillean modern movement. Richard Neutra's visits to the island in 1943 allowed local professionals to have direct contact with one of the leaders of the European avant-garde: Henry Klumb, Osvaldo Toro, Miguel Ferrer, and Luis Torregrosa collaborated with him on the Committee on Design of Public Works. The adoption of a new language, however, did not result in an alternative formal exercise but was based on the functional and technical principles applied in the social projects for schools and hospitals. Invited by Governor Rexford G. Tugwell to serve as a design consultant for Public Works, Neutra elaborated an island-scale plan. It would cost $50 million and was to consist of 150 rural schools, 128 medical centers, and 4 regional hospitals. The rigorous climatological studies, the use of light materials (prefabricated wood), the relationship with nature through the use of terraces and interior patios, and Neutra's mastery in the volumetric articulations and the proportions of spaces comprise a project reference "system" that would impact all the later architecture in the region.

The schools demonstrate Neutra's preoccupation with the way climate and light conditions of the classroom affect children's psychological states. With attention to the research of the Dane Arne Jacobsen, Neutra studied in detail how to integrate nature into the educational space. The typical classroom of Corona School (1935) and the Emerson Junior High School (1938) reappear in Puerto Rico with a wall that replaces the expensive sliding metallic carpentry: here, pivoting wood panels totally open the outer wall toward the garden. The

Mario Romañach,
Jose Noval Cueto
Residence Country Club,
Havana,
1949–51.
Photo by Eduardo Luis
Rodriguez.

Union Headquarters,
Fort-de-France, Martinique,
1930–40.

Albert Mangones,
office building,
Port-au-Prince, Haiti,
1940–50.

Antonio de Caro,
Faculty of Medicine,
Ciudad Universitaria,
Santo Domingo,
1935.

Leo and Marcial Pou Ricart,
Salomé Ureña de Henríquez school,
Santo Domingo,
1943.

Jorge Ramirez de Arellano,
El Falansterio housing,
Puerta de Tierra,
San Juan, Puerto Rico,
1935.

functional study of the district hospitals of varying dimensions is also quite rigorous, they were planned for Caguas, Ponce, Guyama, and Mayagüez. Although only the small primary school was built, the seed left by Neutra bloomed in the work of its disciples, led by Henry Klumb (1905–84), who came from the United States and established his home definitively on the island.

The assimilation of new codes was not easy for local professionals, who were still attached to the academic heritage or to neocolonial historicism. For example, Pedro Méndez Mercado, one of the architects with great professional success in this period, worked for a year with Richard Neutra and Henry Klumb on the Committee on Design of Public Works and soon moved away because he did not identify with the methodology of design applied in the studio. The social housing plans executed in San Juan—San Agustín and San Antonio (1940), Las Acacias in Puerta de Tierra (1949–50), and Puerto Nuevo Norte—and in the rural areas, promoted by North American companies, repeat stereotyped schemes of blocks of reinforced concrete or prefabricated elements devoid of aesthetic value.[25] An exception is the Falansterio in Puerta de Tierra (1938), designed by Jorge Ramirez de Arellano with a series of articulated inner plazas between the three-story blocks that create social spaces used by the community. The careful proportions of the buildings and the treatment of the facades with Art Deco motifs give it a cultural value that was not maintained in the later anonymous *caseríos* (groups of houses) made by the State.[26]

We have already made mention of the existence of extreme double standards accepted by the Trujillo regime in the Dominican Republic: on one hand, the canonical rationalism of Guillermo González; on the other, the fascist monumentalism of Henry Gazón Bona. Nevertheless, the works commissioned by the government in 1943–44 to commemorate the centennial of the republic created opportunities for the architects identified with the modern movement. With varying degrees of coherence, in orthodox terms or tinged with Art Deco or monumentalist elements, the rationalist vocabulary is present in diverse social works in Santo Domingo. The Salomé Ureña de Henriquez School (1943) by Leo and Marcial Pou Ricart, influenced by the Dutch works of J. J. P. Oud, is one of the most creative and unitary examples in terms of the articulation of interior spaces; a centripetal movement is generated in the circular lobby at the entrance. Other noteworthy examples include the Quarter of Civil Firemen, the horse racetrack Perla Antillana, and the Güibia Casino by González and José Antonio Caro. In the same period, Caro and Leo Pou Ricart realized the tracing of the Ciudad Universitaria (University Campus), and the first buildings— the Faculty of Medicine, followed by the Alma Mater (head office)—were constructed according to the design by Humberto Ruiz Castillo that was permeated by academicism. This language reappeared in the Education Secretary by Caro and culminated in the Palace of Justice of Ciudad Nueva by Mario Lluberes. In the urban landscape, the rationalism prevailed over monumental models, demonstrating the architects' freedom in reaching "soft" solutions suited to the tropical climate and Antillean taste.

In Cuba, from the late 1930s to the early 1950s, the State was particularly involved in buildings for education and public health. There are common elements that characterize the evolution of the formal codes, from the monumentalism of the Anti-Tuberculosis Sanatorium (1937) in Topes de Collantes by Miguel Angel Moenck and Enrique Luis Varela to the compositional looseness of Radiocentro Building (1947/49) in Havana by Emilio de Junco, Miguel Gastón, and Martín Domínguez. An attachment to Beaux-Arts axial compositions and symmetrical structures slowly loosens up to the contemporary compositional freedom; on the exterior, the principal access is signaled by monumental or decorative attributes (Art Deco details or sculptures); functionality is exteriorized through continuous horizontal railings and carpentry, as well as the adoption of curved elements taken from yacht style. For interior spaces, dissimilar materials—marble and granite—are used with a modern expression: the smooth planes, the winding curvature of the stairs, and the integration with the light fixtures.

The contrast between traditionalists and innovators is evident in the competition for the Anti-Tuberculosis Sanatorium (1937). In the winning project, by Moenck and Varela, the monumental scheme imposes itself in aggressive form over the mountainous landscape without any dialogue. In other submissions by Emilio de Soto and Armando Pujol y Moya, there is, on the contrary, an attempt to articulate the volumetric components to attenuate the giant scale of the building.

Academic vision weakens other projects, both winners of the Gold Medal of the National College of Architects: the Angel Aballí Children's Hospital (1937, awarded in 1944) by Luis Dauval and the Workers' Maternity Hospital of Marianao (1939, awarded in 1942) by Emilio de Soto. In both cases, the horizontal structure of the composition prevails over the verticality of the symbolic attributes of the access. The thickness of the volumes is indicated by the curved Mendelsohnian balconies that define the "edge" of the building.

As of 1944, the government of Grau San Martín envisioned building plans on a country scale, and the ensuing projects for provincial hospitals and institutes of secondary education have designs that come close to the International Style, which spread from the United States after World War II. Among these works, the Veterinary School of the Havana University by Manuel de Tapia Ruano (1945) stands out, due to the planimetric freedom arising from seizing the site's irregular form

Emilio de Soto,
Workers' Maternity Hospital,
Havana,
1939.

Ministerio de Obras Publicas (MOP)
with Mario Romañach, Antonio Quintana,
and Pedro Martínez Inclán,
Workers' Residential Park in Luyanó, Havana,
1945.

Max Borges Recio,
Surgical Medical Center,
Havana,
1948.

Junco, Gastón, and Domínguez,
Radiocentro Building,
Havana,
1947.

and from the articulation of the functions around an inner patio. A qualitative jump occurs in three Cuban works that demonstrate how the teachings of Gropius, Sert, and Breuer were assimilated through their first built works in North America: the Miramar clinic by Rafael de Cárdenas, the Surgical Medical Center (winner of the Gold Medal in 1948) by Max Borges Recio and the Radio, Cinematography and Television Center, or CMQ (Radiocentro, 1947), in the Vedado neighborhood of Havana, by Junco, Gastón, and Domínguez. According to Nicolás Quintana, the radio center is as significant for Havana as the Ministry of Education and Health is for Rio de Janeiro. The academic references are definitely left behind; the accents and axial composite systems: each function manifests itself with an identified volume that is articulated at an urban scale over the unevenness of the land and the accentuation of the circulatory system integrated into the surrounding streets. Thus we already find ourselves in the 1950s generation that was to open a fertile and creative decade of Cuban architecture.

It is possible to conclude this panorama of State works in Cuba with the only social housing block constructed in Havana within the CIAM urbanism canons: the Workers' Residential Park of Luyanó (1945). Fifteen hundred individual houses were planned—although only 177 were built—in eight four-story apartment blocks with diverse social services: a school, a free market, a home for senior citizens, and wide green areas with sport facilities.[27] The small houses repeated the design schemes accepted by low-income groups (the compact parallelogram with the entryway in the front), yet in the blocks, the expressive resources of the stairs and the exterior circulations were exploited by the young designers Mario Romañach and Antonio Quintana, in terms of plastic expression. The demand expressed by the avant-garde— to attain an urban image more suitable to social necessities—obtained in these works its minimum expression: proof of a desire impossible to realize within the prevailing political system.

Notes

1. Roberto Segre, *Arquitectura Antillana del Siglo XX* (Bogota-Havana: Universidad Nacional de Colombia, Editorial Arte y Literatura, 2003), 176.

2. Eduardo Luis Rodríguez, *The Havana Guide: Modern Architecture, 1925–1965* (New York: Princeton University Press), xviii.

3. Alberto Camacho, "Nuevas tendencias arquitectónicas," in *Colégio de Arquitectos de La Habana* 12, no. 6 (July 1928): 7.

4. Joaquín E. Weiss, "Balance de la arquitectura contemporánea. In memoriam del profesor Alberto Camacho y Llovet," *Arquitectura y Artes Decorativas* 16, no. 7/8 (October/November 1932): 9.

5. Joaquín E. Weiss, *El Rascacielos* (Havana: Molina y Cía, 1934).

6. Angel Guido, *La Maquinolatrie de Le Corbusier* (Rosario: Author Edition, 1929).

7. Adolf Max Vogt, *Le Corbusier, the Noble Savage: Towards an Archaeology of Modernism* (Cambridge, Mass.: MIT Press, 1998).

8. Carmen A. Rivera de Figueroa, *Architecture for the Tropics: A Bibliographical Synthesis* (San Juan: Editorial Universitaria, 1980), 27.

9. Alejo Carpentier, *Crónicas*, vol. 1 (Havana: Editorial de Arte y Literatura, 1975), 271.

10. Eric Mumford, *The CIAM Discourse on Urbanism 1928–1960* (Cambridge, Mass: MIT Press, 2000), 128.

11. Nicolás Quintana, "Evolución histórica de la arquitectura en Cuba," in *Enciclopedia de Cuba* (Madrid: Playor, 1974), 5:94, and Nicolás Quintana, "Cuba en su arquitectura y urbanismo. Pasado. Los años 50. Presente y futuro," in *AAA, Archivos de Arquitectura Antillana* 5, no. 10 (June 2000): 146–55.

12. Ramón Gutiérrez, *Arquitectura y Urbanismo en Iberoamérica* (Madrid: Ediciones Cátedra, 1983), 583.

13. Eduardo Subirats, *A Penúltima Visão do Paraíso. Ensaios sobre Memória e Globalização* (São Paulo: Studio Nobel, 2001), 138.

14. Iván A. Rodríguez and Margot Ammidown, *From Wilderness to Metropolis: The History and Architecture of Dade County, Florida, 1825–1940* (Miami: Metropolitan Dade County, 1982), 153.

15. Eduardo Tejeira-Davis, *Roots of Modern Latin American Architecture. The Hispano-Caribbean Region from the Late 19th Century to the Recent Past* (Heidelberg: Heidelberg University, 1987), 360.

16. Selden Rodman, *Haiti: The Black Republic* (Old Greenwich, Conn.: Devin-Adair, 1973), 91.

17. Pérez-Chanis, "Génesis y ruta de la arquitectura en Puerto Rico," *La Gran Enciclopedia de Puerto Rico*, vol. 9 (Madrid: Ediciones R, 1976), 92.

18. Willy Boesiger, *Buildings and Projects by Richard Neutra* (Zurich: Éditions Girsberger, 1951), 114.

19. Richard Neutra, *Architecture of Social Concern in Regions of Mild Climate* (São Paulo: G. Todtmann, 1948) and Richard Neutra, *Survival through Design* (New York: Oxford University Press, 1954).

20. Lillian Llanes, *Apuntes para una historia sobre los constructores cubanos* (Havana: Editorial Letras Cubanas, 1985), 75.

21. Eduardo Luis Rodríguez, *La Habana. Arquitectura del siglo XX* (Barcelona: Blume, 1998), 240.

22. Joaquín E. Weiss, *Arquitectura cubana contemporánea* (Havana: Colégio Nacional de Arquitectos, Cultural, 1947), 66.

23. Maria Luisa Lobo Montalvo, *Havana: History and Architecture of a Romantic City* (New York: Monacelli Press, 2000), 275–82.

24. Roberto Segre, "La Habana. Ortodoxia y digresiones de la Primera Modernidad," in *Arquitectura en la Ciudad de La Habana. Primera Modernidad*, by R. Segre and C. Sambricio (Madrid: Electa, 2000), 72.

25. Samuel E. Bleecker, *The Politics of Architecture: A Perspective on Nelson A. Rockefeller.* (New York: Rutledge Press, 1981).

26. Aníbal Sepúlveda and Jorge Carbonell, *San Juan Extramuros. Iconografía para su estudio* (San Juan: Centro de Investigaciones Carimar, Oficina Estatal de Preservación Histórica, 1990), 59.

27. Joseph Scarpaci, Roberto Segre, and Mario Coyula, *Havana: Two Faces of the Antillean Metropolis* (Chapel Hill: University of North Carolina Press, 2002), 76.

SEGRE

ROUNDTABLE DISCUSSION

Left to right
Seated:
Ruth Verde Zein
Mario Ganelsonas
Jorge Francisco Liernur
Paulina Villanueva
Kenneth Frampton

Standing:
Lauro Cavalcanti
Terence Riley
Monica Ponce de Leon
Carlos Brillembourg
José Antonio Aldrete-Haas
Enrique Norten
Rafael Viñoly

Terence Riley

Mario Gandelsonas, Professor of Architecture at Princeton University and Principal of Agrest & Gandelsonas Architects here in New York, will be leading the panel discussion. He'll be giving some remarks on format. In addition to Professor Gandelsonas: Paulina Villanueva, Professor of Architecture, Universidad Central, Caracas; Monica Ponce de Leon, Principal, Office dA, and Associate Professor of Architecture at Harvard University; Rafael Viñoly, Principal, Rafael Viñoly Architects, New York; Ruth Verde Zein, architect, critic, and Professor of Architecture, MacKenzie University, São Paulo; and Enrique Norten, architect, TEN Arquitectos, Mexico City. Let's welcome them all.

Mario Gandelsonas

Thank you, Terry. I was asked to introduce this session, so I'll try to be quite brief and bring up some issues that I think might complicate the debate. It hasn't been easy for me to put together this text. And I'm going to let you know why. When I received Terry Riley's letter, inviting me to participate in this symposium, my first instinct was to decline. I feel that I'm not an expert in Latin American architecture. I have seen only a few buildings, and the issues are quite distant from my preoccupations and my practice. I do know a little bit about Argentina, but that's about it. I have visited almost every country in the Americas but never examined Latin American architecture in a systematic way. The present political and economic situation in Latin America in general, and in Argentina in particular, added to the sense of uneasiness when I thought that we would be discussing what Frampton called, in his preface to the book *Latin American Architecture: Six Voices,* a marginal practice, an anachronism. However, the impossibility for architecture to solve the disastrous economic situation and the chaotic political landscape does not imply that there isn't a role for architecture. I feel deeply that architecture can do more for Latin America than the loans provided by the IMF, which are basically destined to pay back previous loans, as we know, and not to improve the desperate conditions of those countries. Architecture can bring poetry, beauty, and reflection. Not to mention comfort. And perhaps even a sense of place. It's precisely for this reason that I decided to accept the invitation. You can call it solidarity. Of course, not all architectural practice can provide these things. Some of them, for the particular way in which they operate in the Third World, feel to me closer to those IMF loans. But that is a potential subject for a different conference. [LAUGHTER] Since I knew that MoMA had organized in the past two exhibitions and published two books, I decided to start my education on Latin America by reading these books. Published, as you probably know, in the forties and fifties. The first one, *Brazil Builds,* referred to by Lauro [Cavalcanti] and published in

1943 on the occasion of the first examination of Latin American architecture by MoMA, I really enjoyed. On that occasion, the architect Philip Goodwin flew to Brazil with Peter Smith, as he says, armed with a Zeiss Juwel A camera. They traveled with a dual purpose: on one hand, they were anxious to establish a close relationship, and I am quoting, "with a country that was to be a future ally of the U.S." On the other hand, they were extremely interested in examining Brazilian architecture. Not just for its creativity, but for pragmatic reasons as well—to know more about their solutions to the problem of controlling heat and light on large exterior glass surfaces. This pragmatism, this Realpolitik at the time of war, sounded perfectly okay to me. I didn't find any problem with an exhibition that attempted to show North Americans the "charming" old and the "inspiring" new buildings in Brazil. The new architecture that, according to Goodwin, extended to all parts of the world "has the character of the country and the architects who designed it. Second, it fits its climate and the materials for which it is intended. Third, it has carried the evolution of the whole movement some steps forward toward full development of the ideas launched in Europe and America. Brazil has launched out in an adventurous but inevitable course. The rest of the world can admire what has been done and look forward to still finer things as time goes on." However, my second read, the second book, *A Survey of Latin American Architecture* by Henry-Russell Hitchcock, who visited eleven countries in Latin America and selected forty-six buildings, I found deeply troubling. Under the label Latin American architecture, the book flattens the differences, in my view, looking only at built objects and potential star architects who push the development of modern architecture. In particular, the book ignores the incredibly rich cultural context of Argentina (and obviously that touches me directly), where architecture was just one of a multiplicity of artistic practices. Since I'm not a historian, I don't need to play objectively. He shows a building by [Antonio] Bonet and a house by [Amancio] Williams, the house that Pancho Liernur just showed us. However, he's blind to Bonet's surreal atelier . . . or to the structural inventiveness of [Eduardo] Catalano's structural experiments. He's blind to architecture that is not just a building, but a debate of ideas, that is, an experimental urbanism—architecture as a field where daring structural accomplishments were implemented. Obviously, the engineers were not in his field of vision. Well, that's one of the reasons why he ignores Argentina's complex and vibrant culture. A theoretical battlefield between different tendencies that created the space of artistic, architectural, and urban experimentation of which Liernur has shown, even to me, an unknown aspect. In fact, at that point Argentina represents a search for both global connections and local identity, obviously reflecting the vision of the ruling class, but perhaps a model for future reflection of the multiplicity of internal cultures that coexist in that country. What's being said is determined, in Henry-Russell Hitchcock's book, by what is not being said. In this case, what's not being said is the political agenda. And we all know the lack of sympathy for the Perón regime's anti-U.S. policies and the lack of interest in intellectual speculation and in nonofficial art, like surrealism, originally connected to Marxism, or the concretely anti-creative, scientific, concrete art. And that touches me directly because I was a witness—now we're getting to my autobiographical section—I was a witness in the late fifties and throughout the sixties to this incredible cultural scene that started in the forties and culminated in the sixties. Nineteen fifty-seven to 1967 were my formative years in Buenos Aires, when I had direct experience of this unique period of cultural effervescence. I spent most of my time during the late fifties and early sixties moving back and forth from the Nueva Vision building, located on Cerrito and Alvear, next to the Jockey Club, the epicenter of the Argentinian ruling class, to the Laboratory of Electronic Music, which was located in the School of Architecture, where I was completing my studies. In the Nueva Vision building, where the Victoria House was located, I worked as an intern in the office of Francisco Bullrich and his partner, Alicia Cazzaniga. They were part of the group Organization of Modern Architecture (OAM) when they were working on the competition for the national library with Clorindo Testa, who had been my teacher. I couldn't wait for the next issue of the magazine *Nueva Vision.* . . . I was studying music, . . . helping with the organization of the Association of New Music, which met monthly on the third floor of that same building to discuss the schedule of concerts. And then of course, what's memorable for me were the five-o'clock teas of the Organization of Modern Architecture. There, visitors from the U.S. and Europe would bring the latest news. The most anticipated occasion was Maldonado's annual visit to Argentina from Ulm, where he was directing the school. And then of course in the sixties, we shifted to a different context within the school of architecture, to the seminars organized by César Janello on structuralism and semiotics. The debates on Archigram and Cedric Price, and my introduction to the American artistic avant-garde through the Museum of Modern Art. And of course, because this is about high culture, I'm not mentioning here the Beatles, the Rolling Stones, and pot. It was primarily the fluidity and the relationships between the different artistic practices. The way they fed and inspired each other gave me the feeling of living in a vital center, or perhaps rather in a node connected to other nodes, that triangulated in my imagination Buenos Aires with the U.S. and Europe.

Thinking about that time, I realized that the relatively small cultural context of Buenos Aires, linked to Europe and the U.S. with a limited number of artists and architects engaged in this movement of discussions and production, made this interaction possible. It was not until I came to New York, first in 1967, and then again in 1970 and '71 to stay, that I first confronted and discovered the notion of Argentina as a Latin American country. [LAUGHTER] Actually, Argentina was definitely on the way to becoming a prime example of the economic and political failure that is usually associated with Latin America—of successive dictatorships, of countless *desaparecidos,* that is, the disappeared, of emulating the worst nightmares that its neighbor, Chile, lived with after the Pinochet coup. Today I can only bring my own experience of one period, the beginning of the second half of the twentieth century. The experience of only one country, Argentina. Of only one city, Buenos Aires. A place where Duchamp spent eight months, since we're kind of nostalgic. Duchamp came in 1970, stayed for eight months, started to work with silver on glass. (By the way, Argentina means the country of silver, *argento*.) I just wanted to talk about Duchamp and Corbusier because they hated each other. A place of entry for Corbusier, when he came to South America for the first time in 1929, invited by Victorio Campo, and closed his first period of white houses. That's basically to clarify a passage in Frampton's presentation when he mentioned [the book] *Precisions*, but he didn't mention that that actually took place in Buenos Aires. So I just wanted to make sure that everybody knows that that is where it took place, and not in Rio. [LAUGHTER] I'm convinced that the cultural energy that I knew is still there, and that it's producing, at this very moment, powerful art, if not great architecture, which unfortunately always requires some sort of healthy and perhaps power- ful economy. Latin American countries have been and still are economic and political failures. But they have never been cultural failures. Every one of the countries subsumed under the label Latin America, in my view, has the potential for the highest level of artistic and architectural production, like the one I just described, which will probably be very different from the story I just told you, but will be great material for future stories. [APPLAUSE] So now that I hope I've fully changed the tone a bit [LAUGHTER] I would like you all to give me your comments. They say struc- turally you're supposed to be respondents, but I would also like to free up your roles. In a way, this was a way of provoking you into some personal stories perhaps. So, yes, you go first.

Paulina Villanueva

When Carlos Brillembourg invited me to participate in this event, the first thing that I asked myself was, Why do we meet today, at the beginning of a new century, trying to review, from a contemporary perspective, the period of Latin American architecture between 1929 and 1960? It is very significant that MoMA organized this event, since the museum has been characterized by its outstanding work as a leader of reflection and debate in the field of architecture. Modern and Latin American architecture have been central topics to this effort. And we have to remember the *Modern Architecture International Exhibition*, organized in 1932, which showed some of the most significant examples of European architecture at that moment. Also the great significance of the 1942 and 1955 exhibitions, *Brazil Builds* and *Latin American Architecture since 1945.*

Then I asked myself another question: Why we are not discussing today, as we did in 1955, the [present] vitality and the new proposals for Latin American architecture? We probably feel uncertainty. We are not as enthusiastic as we were then. And when this happens, it is not bad to look back. And also, in looking back, I think that we must recognize a singular, temporary paradox. We are trying to discover our future in our past. On the other hand, it is necessary to say that this period of modern architecture has great significance in any debate about architecture. We cannot overcome the condition of being simply "the after." And we remain with a bitter taste . . . and everything, or almost everything, for better or worse, has [already] been thought, said, or done. In the same sense, Le Corbusier continues to be the architect paradigm. And it is with good reason that Kenneth Frampton calls him "architect of the twentieth century." And it is precisely Corbusier who fixes indirectly the beginning and ending of the period that is the object of this meeting today. The year 1929 is when he first traveled to South America and 1960, when he wrote the introduction for the reprint of *Precisions*, the book in which he compiled the ten Buenos Aires speeches. However, inside the wide spectrum that modern architecture and Le Corbusier offer, there could be different perspectives of approximation. And I want to distinguish two, form and content.

Modern architecture was part of a plastic revolution without precedence. Achieving a new language, a new and complex language, for the architecture was one of its main principles. The progress toward establishing a new formal vocabulary was made real with the use of new materials and techniques. . . . Moreover, it is good to remember two things: first, that this battle wasn't fought by architecture alone, isolated from other arts. In Argentina in 1951, the magazine *Nueva Vision,* published by Tomás Maldonado, is a good example. Reviewing the content of the first issues, we can understand its pedagogic vocation toward a new visual culture. And we can see how artists— such as Moholy-Nagy, Albers, Klee, Mondrian, Van der Leck, Kandinsky, or Arp—are next to Amancio Williams, Francisco Bullrich, Richard Neutra, Jorge Romero-Brest, or Pierre Francastel. This coincidence of interest between art and architecture has a fundamental weight in the Latin American architecture of this period. In the specific case of my father, I can state that it is impossible to understand his work using only the field of modern European architecture as a reference.

A second consideration is the adjustment and transformation of that language when it crosses the silence of the ocean and reaches American territory. In his American prologue, Le Corbusier speaks insistently about geography, landscape, and climate: the tropical summer, the magnificent sun, the palms, the red land, the sand, the beaches, the mountains, the plains, and especially the light—this immense light that makes him exclaim, "Under this light architecture will be born." And in this respect, Brazil, with its immense geography, is a clear example of how American territory gave birth to a formal exuberance that had no parallel in Europe. However, America is more. And the cultural context of the different Latin American countries produces a formal *mestizaje* particular to each place. In some, as is the case of Mexico, the weight of the pre-Hispanic and colonial culture was of cardinal importance in the formation of a new language. In others, as in the case of Venezuela, it was the influence of a modest colonial Spanish architecture, fundamentally domestic, which was used as a fragile reference before the blind leap of faith—that meant, for Venezuela, a transition toward modernity without passing through the intermediate stage that other countries experienced in their development. But it would be unforgivable to consider modern architecture from an exclusively plastic point of view. The formal cannot be isolated from the context that stimulated deep cultural renovation. The form was, for modern architecture, the most valuable instrument in the reconstruction of a way of life. The architecture was a cause, not simply a style. And this architecture acquires a new scale and a new meaning by means of its fundamental social commitment.

In this cause, Corbusier has a singular role. Five years before his death, Corbusier reaffirmed what he understood: to place today's man in an environment of daily happiness, to establish the harmony between the man and his environment. And it was precisely in this utopian aspiration that the force and the weakness of modern architecture reside. Architecture is caught in its existential condition of projection toward a society that does not yet exist. Importantly, this society never came to be. Now, we have to understand what happened after. The utopia gave way to fantasy. And if the utopia is a commitment that points to the collective thing and looks ahead, fantasy answers to individual longings. It is essentially conservative and devoid of commitment. Guided by fantasy, our "after" has been converted into an accumulation of gestures and form without content. Within the difficult perspective of contemporary architecture, Latin American countries are immersed in tremendous economic and social upheaval. . . . We have become accustomed to a society without time or space. . . . Facing a society like this raises two possibilities—protest and utopia. And I dare say that they are the only two possibilities. And to construct a new utopia, we have to rethink the relationship between man and architecture, between architecture and reality, and this is not an easy task. Therefore, we need courage and determination, and to give you hope I repeat to you a request that was made by my father in 1962 when he dealt with the new problems that architecture had to face. He said, "The final recommendation that I will make here is one of old. We shall try to be, from now on, worthy of our future." **[APPLAUSE]**

Rafael Viñoly

I think the most compelling part of the statement that Mario [Gandelsonas] put forth a moment ago is basically how you mix these things on a personal level and how you interpret the conditions of politics and how you operate. And since I was at this five-o'clock tea, the guy who was going out and buying the cookies for these people to eat, I had the perspective of an observer on that phenomenal period. But also, in my own sort of silent way, a critic, too. I was born in Uruguay. And in a way, my whole tradition of engagement in architecture comes from the peculiarities of Montevideo, which I'm told you were shown this morning. Nevertheless, my connection to Argentina, which is much longer, is really significant. But at the same time, I did spend three years of my life in Brazil, too. So if for no other reason than I presume that I'm the only one who can offer you a little bit of that perspective, I will tell you what I think about all of this rehashing of the past.

Mario mentioned the question of the ruling class and the apparent disconnection between the effervescence and the importance of cultural development [on the one hand] and [on the other] the way in which a very peculiar bourgeoisie appropriated, and still appropriates, approximately 38 percent of the total gross national product of the country. In Argentina, there are no more than sixteen families, the so-called groups, that actually hold that level of ownership. Because of that and because at the end of the day, they never really had to work, they basically had time to entertain themselves with a number of beautiful things. I am not resentful about that. I just think that it is a completely different way to see Corbusier's trip to Argentina. . . . (By the way, I don't know how many of you know that he disappeared for a week, and nobody knows where he was. That would be interesting to figure it out.) **[LAUGHTER]**

But the other important part of the trip was that he was actually chasing a job. And at any expense. . . . It is really revealing to see the correspondence between Corbusier and Silvina Ocampo and Victoria Ocampo—on the expectations for a job, the frustration because this lady didn't give him a job. The disappearance at a very particular point because he actually was scheduled to give two conversations at her *salon* in Buenos Aires. And nothing wrong with getting a job, I think it's just great. But to confuse the getting of a job with a kind of cultural mission is a little bit of a stretch to me. And I think that he went to get a job in Brazil, and because Brazil is a country (and I can testify to this and I'm sure that Ruth [Verde Zein] would agree in the end) that has a much more important quota of self-possessedness and never really quite thought that Avenida de Mayo was Madrid. Or that Palermo was Paris. They really cut him off completely, and they did, in my view, ten times better than what he could have done, a lot of beautiful and important things. So that accounts for Hitchcock coming back and looking at all of that. Because in the end they had a promise, which is a very European notion, and then these so-called poor guys, who by the way have a great sense of humor and an enormous amount of integration with their own geography, climate, and particular culture, took exactly what they needed to take. And what they needed to take from him was, in my view, not so much the formal system, but in a way what he permitted, which was legitimizing a certain unstoppable process of liberating the culture from two things, which to me are really pivotal here. One is the traditional, which is fragmented, *mal* copied, I mean, poorly copied and totally unsubstantial, but nevertheless associated with the level of power that most of the bourgeoisie really held dear. And the second was the fact that the independence of thinking was something that was precluded at a much more rooted level. It is remarkable that there are two letters about his stay in Buenos Aires and his short trip to Uruguay. Several people organized the competition, which was supposed to be won by Corbusier and it really was not secret. I mean, it was nothing confidential. It was the replanning of the city of Mendoza in Argentina. The competition was not won by Corbusier but by another fabulous architect in Montevideo. By the way, all Uruguayans, including myself, have a very limited sense of humor, compared with people in Brazil, who enjoy life a lot more. [LAUGHTER] So this gentleman, Corbusier, wrote a very, very interesting letter, which is in the annals of the School of Architecture in Uruguay—an absolutely wonderful building that I recommend visiting—explaining why this competition, like so many others—I mean, we were talking about Aldo Rossi a minute ago, he did it too—explaining to the jury, the government, and everybody else why he had to win it. And if you put the letters to Victoria, the letter to the government of Mendoza, and the answer that the winning architect wrote in defense of his plan, you would understand what, to me, is one of the most significant problems in Latin America. I think that we all are on the same boat for this one, on the absolutely lethal consequences of Hispanic education. Savonarola had actually been dead for a long time, but he was probably revived around Argentina. [Note] the level of frustration in a system of education that is completely geared toward the fabrication of layers of authority, some of which are well deserved, some of which are completely fake. And I would dare to say that most of them are completely fake, and perhaps the best example is the reading of the political situation in Latin America in institutional times. You know, Chavez, Mr. Duarte, Mr. Menem before the attempts in Uruguay to really become a financial center of an economic system that was actually primarily selling the assets through the participation of this level of complicity, which I think is, in the end, much more significant than any moments of brilliance that could appear. So in my mind, it is not possible to disassociate the reading of these moments of absolutely brilliant production from the conditions under which [they are produced], and that may explain, to a certain extent, why the future is so far away.

Mario Gandelsonas

Thank you, Rafael. [APPLAUSE]

Monica Ponce de Leon

I'm in charge of responding to Carlos Brillembourg's presentation. And I think instead of responding to his presentation, I would like to expand on the topic a little bit further. For me, the work of Villanueva poses particular questions regarding the global dissemination and implementation of the general precepts of the modern movement in Latin America. As we have seen in only a few hours, in Latin America, the language of modernity has had very different histories and different incarnations. Its meaning, purpose, and the way that it came about actually vary greatly according to the specific sociopolitical realities of each country. While the International Style was imported to almost every corner of the Americas, its survival in each nation was neither simultaneous, nor even the same. Now, I think understanding the specific tension between modernity and national identity gives a more complex picture of the changing role that the modern movement came to play in Central and South America. There is more to architecture in Latin America than the so-called modern movement. In Venezuela, the arrival of the International Style was paradoxical. Modernity arrived in Caracas at a time when a political reaction against foreign influences was actually paralleled in architecture by a mythical return to Hispanicity, which is of course the revival of colonial architecture, and later by a return to local traditions, vernacular architecture. At the same time, the modern movement developed in Venezuela without the context of the Industrial Revolution. Mass production and means of communication were virtually absent in Caracas. Architects had to contend with a severe lack of technology and had to be content with building the effects of modernity. Between 1930 and 1950—and, one has to remember, under three different governments—Venezuelan architecture developed among contradictory tendencies that aimed at incorporating elements from another culture, which was considered somehow more advanced, and at the same time, searching to embody an intangible national tradition. Now, by the end of the fifties these paradoxes had run their course, playing out very differently depending on the social groups to which architecture was aiming to cater. Villanueva played a crucial role in the resolution, or lack thereof, of these issues.

I think it's important to stress that he dedicated himself almost exclusively to public works. This is important because it is in public works that the relationship between architecture and social change was potentially more intimately related. By doing so, he opened the door for the International Style's association with a collective image of the nation; a nation searching for an identity of its own somehow finds it in modernity. Now, in his early public projects, Villanueva followed stylistic roles that were then expected in institutional buildings. But we know that this was not a stylistic period for him because at the same time he built a house in the International Style in the suburbs of Caracas. This lack of gradual transformation from one style to the next—and instead the strategic use of traditional imagery when necessary—has led to the interpretation that Villanueva may have postponed dealing with modernity as a conscious decision, waiting to gain respect as an architect before introducing new forms to the architectural vocabulary. It was in his next two public projects, as we saw with the example of El Silencio that Carlos [Brillembourg] presented, that Villanueva searched for a connection between colonial architecture and the International Style. Now, Villanueva saw no contradiction between the modern movement and neoclassical local traditions. While other architects and thinkers of the time saw modernity as a threat to what was typically Venezuelan, Villanueva explored colonial architecture as having a rational spirit and thus somehow being in accordance with modernity. In his book *Caracas En Tres Tiempos*, which means Caracas in Three Periods, he traces the history of colonial architecture, culminating in the El Silencio project. Also, most important, in his essay "The Reason of Our Colonial Architecture," he does a functional analysis of the elements that are typical of the colonial city. Now for Villanueva, El Silencio was the beginning of what would become one of his central preoccupations— how to respond to the housing needs of the large numbers of rural workers who, in the forties and fifties, were flocking from the countryside to the city. The social housing projects that followed, which we didn't see today (El Paradiso, 23 de Enero), were the perfect setting for testing the ideal urban process of CIAM. Villanueva was able to take advantage of the government's eagerness to define a new image for itself at a time of relative wealth. Of course, underlying this government campaign was the desire to hide the realities of the slums that populated the hills of Caracas, a reality that negated the imaged of prosperity that Pérez Jiménez's dictatorship wanted to portray. The housing problem, however, was very real, as was the need for a source of labor for these rural masses. The general was young and inexperienced, putting into practice largely theoretical models. This utopia soon came to be confronted with the social reality of the moment. An underdeveloped country without social institutions or long-term programs led to difficulties in the maintenance and upkeep of the housing projects, and in adaptations from the farming life to apartment living.

Now, Villanueva's work for the government entered its most significant chapter with the University City project. The idea of incorporating into an entire university campus the work of national and international artists, transforming the campus into an open museum, might seem socially appropriate for us today, but at the time it was a radical move.

It is clear that with the university, Pérez Jiménez was aiming to acquire prestige in the eyes of intellectuals as well as political recognition at home and abroad. This was compounded by the fact that the grand opening of the University Central Area (Aula Magna, covered patio, and the main library) was orchestrated to coincide with the opening of the tenth Ibero-American Conference. The conference was attended by representatives from all American states, as well as the U.S. Secretary of State. And the conference actually gave further legitimacy to the government of Pérez Jiménez. Now, Villanueva had bigger fishes to fry, so to speak. He understood the political strategy and took advantage of it. He selected and acquired as many works of art as possible before the event, understanding that as soon as the conference was over, the government would turn its interest to other areas. And, indeed, acquiring works for the university seems to have been a priority. . . .

In this way, Villanueva was able to amass for this so-called Third World public university—and I think the public aspect of this is important to stress—a first-class international collection. Also, Villanueva was able to give voice to a new generation of Venezuelan artists who, at the time, were at the margins of the Venezuelan cultural production, where figuration still occupied a privileged position and abstraction was derided. So I believe that the kind of historical analysis that Carlos Brillembourg presented today, an analysis that moves us away from formalist interpretations of the European influence in Latin America, is precisely the kind of analysis needed to help us better understand Latin America in the context of a globalization, a globalization that I would argue started in Latin America almost one hundred years ago.

And I would like to finish on a personal note. As the daughter of Spanish immigrants, I grew up traveling extensively in Europe, in the U.S., and in South America. And I have to confess that while growing up, all of the world looked just the same to me. When

I was twelve years old, I went to the Aula Magna for the first time (to be onstage as a member of a choral group, I'm embarrassed to say). And I remember vividly feeling that I had entered a space unlike any that I had ever seen before, and I was not surprised at all to find that at home. I was not surprised to find that this place was produced in Venezuela. We did a terrible job singing, and I did not become a singer, and I eventually moved to Miami and I pursued architectural studies and so on. [LAUGHTER] And to me, Miami seemed the Third World in comparison to Caracas. Thank you. [APPLAUSE]

Mario Gandelsonas

Ruth, Ruth Verde Zein.

Ruth Verde Zein

Thank you for the invitation. I've been here with all of you, and it's been a very nice day. And I was very glad to hear what you said, Monica, for I'm going on the same path, I believe, as Paulina [Villanueva]. For I've asked myself, not why, but what are we going to do about this theme, Latin American Architecture 1930–1960? Again, I think that what we have to do is to broaden and to be precise. And to broaden the narrow limits that have been delimiting the understanding of that architecture. And to be precise about the information by going beyond the superficial knowledge of that architecture. But with ten minutes, all I can do is just point out some things. That's what I'm going to do for Brazilian architecture.

Modern Brazilian architecture is a myth. Contemporary Brazilian architecture is a mystery. [LAUGHTER] What happened after Brasilia? That is the latent question when anyone speaks or writes about the architecture of my great, varied, exuberant country, with its increasingly urbanized population of 130 million people. After being recognized and then publicized in the forties and fifties, Brazilian modern architecture was largely absent from the international journals and magazines for several decades. So any proper understanding of the present state of things must necessarily start from that period. A Herculean task, perhaps doomed to failure if we do not explore anew the multiple meanings of its wide acceptance from the thirties on . . . to modern architecture, this modern architecture affiliated with Le Corbusier, assimilated and transformed mainly by Rio de Janeiro architects, under the intellectual leadership of Lucio Costa. Or [doomed to failure] if we are not sufficiently attentive to other and different influences at work, influences that made up a network of intense complexity that has still not yet been explored in-depth. An engagement with its recent history is also an indispensable requirement for any vision, however rapid and superficial, that intends to shed some light on the most important issues of Brazilian architecture today. The first modern Brazilian—and I would like to be precise now—the first modern Rio de Janeiro architecture, *carioca,* as the people in Rio say, the first modern *carioca,* modern architecture tradition—based on the insights of Lucio Costa, who, with rare fortune combined his academic training with the new teachings of Le Corbusier—is commonly considered absolutely congruent with a sort of mythical, praised, and frozen image of Brazilian modern architecture. Surely it's not quite a wrong assumption. Not at all. It is really beautiful. It's really marvelous. I get emotional every time I go back and see that again. But perhaps that is too hasty and vague an affirmation. For example, the significant changes within Oscar Niemeyer's works during the first half of the fifties and also by the Caracas Museum, which announced new paths that were consolidated in Brasilia, and many other important questions and differences between other local masters, not to mention other interesting and valuable experience from other places in the country. All this cannot be plainly enclosed in the wide and imprecise label "Brazilian Modern"—at the risk of misunderstanding important questions, the very ones that could lead the researcher beyond the limited scope that has until now characterized the established beliefs and ordinary focus on Brazilian architecture. Since his seminal text "Reasons of New Architecture" appeared in 1934, Costa made clear that in assuming modern architecture he was not abandoning certain academic concepts, because for him architecture should be the result of the interrelationship between the composition and character appropriated to the new times. A decade later, he stated that the Brazilian trend of new modern architecture had already matured, mostly through the free and expansive creativity of Oscar Niemeyer, enthroning a single creator as the apex of its image. Surely a political and media coup. While the panorama was being restricted from a group to a person, the rapid acceptance of the new ideas and forms on the part of local architects and architectural professors transformed and inverted its initial and essential achievements. So in a way, the academic tradition, in favor of a limited programmatic functionalist, was conversely complemented by increasing solipsistic and arbitrary formalism. Besides, in such a long time period, from 1930 to 1960, it would be almost impossible to maintain strong and univocal currents within Brazilian modern architecture. There are at least two generations struggling in such a lengthy period. What is more, we can consider other Brazilian regions, not necessarily completely in phase with the *carioca* experience. In order to have a more accurate opinion about Brazilian architecture, the dates should be precise, and the countercurrents and undercurrents, better understood. When working with broader and more precise information, one cannot accept, for instance, that Brazilian architecture culminates and sharply ends a univocal and consistent process. That's crude information, which mostly blurs the panorama, rather than make it understandable. It's true that São Paolo, where I live, played only a secondary role in the sculptural panorama of Brazil until the middle of the twentieth century, with the progressively increasing wealth amassed by the city's rising upper class, first rural, then industrial, and the formation of an extensive proletariat and middle class composed of newcomers from the country and immigrants from abroad. São Paulo assumed a growing importance in the country's economy, accompanied by an even greater importance in cultural terms. It was in the postwar that the country's first two private museums were created, both in São Paulo. In 1948, with the willing support of prosperous local residents, the highly controversial figure of Assis Chateaubriand founded in 1948 the MASP [Museum of Art of São Paulo], with Pietro Maria Bardi as head curator and Lina Bo Bardi as architect. Both of them helped to transform the still-provincial panorama of São Paulo, organizing exhibitions, editing an art and architecture magazine, and designing some of the most significant works of Brazilian architecture over the next three decades, for example, the MASP building on Paulista Avenue. The art scene in the fifties was also polarized between Chateaubriand and his cordial enemy, the Matarazzo family [LAUGHTER], an oil-rich family of recent immigrants from Italy, who, among other initiatives, were responsible for creating the MAM [the Museum of Modern Art] in São Paulo. The Museum of Modern Art of São Paulo immediately sponsored the world-famous São Paulo Art Biennial, which began in 1951 and established the city as a presence in the international arts circuit as well as its appendix, the Architecture Biennial. From 1951 to 1957 the Architecture Biennial of São Paulo received [proposals], exhibited [work], and awarded prizes to such major architects as Le Corbusier, Mies van der Rohe, Walter Gropius, Bruno Zevi, Max Biel, Paul Rudolph, among others, who have contributed to the debate concerning Brazilian architecture, mostly understood as the contributions of the crowning figure of Oscar Niemeyer, actually the designer of the Biennial building and the Parque do Ibirapuera complex in which it has been held from that time on. From 1957 on, the international interest in Brazil was further aroused by the daring enterprise of creating from nothing, in a little more than three years, the new capital, Brasilia. The full and unbiased understanding of the significance of Brasilia as a real-life utopia and the shocking impact it caused are indispensable factors for understanding the subsequent evolution of Brazilian architecture and its progressive distancing from the mainstream of international debate from the sixties on. Soon after Brasilia, the presence of Brazilian architecture receded in international debates.

Brasilia was surely a turning point in the modern movement, not only from the local but also the international standpoint. But there are other significant reasons that contributed to that aloofness, like the conflictive political situation produced by the long military rule imposed on several Latin American countries in the sixties and seventies, causing, as an unwanted byproduct, a decrease in interest in the architecture of these countries. And the rising European wealth after the war and the progressive indifference to former colonies that were decidedly lost by that time.

To end, I must say that Brasilia is not the only interesting product of those years. Although it has never been fully recognized as such by those who created it or even by national or international critics, another architectural avant-garde was being formed in São Paulo in the fifties and expanded and consolidated in the sixties. For lack of a better label, we can name it São Paulo *paulista*, or brutalist, architecture. And the leading figures associated with it include João Batista Villanova Artigas, Paulo Mendes da Rocha, Pedro Paulo de Melo Saraiva, Ruy Ohtake, among others, as well as architects such as Joaquim Guedes. Well to finish, I'll speak on the complexity of Brazilian architecture during at least three generations of architects between the period from 1930 to 1960, which cannot be superficially labeled and reductively underestimated, as has been done since 1960, at least. The panorama is quite complex, but it will never be really understood if the differences are not fully and attentively appreciated. Thank you. [APPLAUSE]

Mario Gandelsonas

Enrique Norten?

Enrique Norten

Thank you. Good afternoon. Unfortunately I don't have a text because I was invited to respond. So I didn't know what I was going to respond to. But unfortunately I also don't have anything to respond to. [LAUGHTER] So what I want to do is, first of all, thank and acknowledge the people who spoke this morning, especially Pancho Liernur and Kenneth Frampton and Lauro Cavalcanti, whom I've never heard before and who gave what I thought was a brilliant presentation of Brazilian architecture. And Carlos Brillembourg as well, especially for bringing to this universal forum names like Niemeyer, Villanueva, Alvarez, Williams, Burle-Marx, Lucio Costa, and for showing us again how important their universality and modernism are. I think it's very important to understand this because they do set up a very solid base for what the people of my generation are now building in America or in the Americas or in Latin America. And I do think that some of the most important examples of contemporary architecture are coming out of Latin America. But anyway, I guess we, at least the architects of my country, are still in debt to the New York audience that was able to show that Barragán was a great modern architect. And I guess we'll have another opportunity to show them without stereotypes or personal anger.

But anyway, I also want to refer to a personal anecdote. One of the last times that I visited Caracas, I had the opportunity to see one of the works that was shown today, which is the Gio Ponti House, which was described today as one of the fantastic works of art. And the lady, Mrs. Planchart, said something that is so true and I think it's very important for understanding this forum. She said, "Well, in order to appreciate modern architecture, you have to be modern." [LAUGHTER] That's something that has been understood by almost everyone this morning. And having said that, I also want to bring up two comments that were made this morning that I thought were very important. One was the invitation that Sondra Farganis made to us to look at the past without nostalgia. The second is that the traditions are only here to be reinvented. And that's what keeps us moving. The dynamic of history is what keeps us moving and keeps our faith in the future. And to understand that present and past are feeding each other constantly. I think all of those bases are absolutely essential to understanding modernity and to understanding modernity in the Americas. And I very much appreciated Terry Riley's phrase, when he mentioned the "new world," which is for sure one of the bastions of modernity of architecture for our generation. That dream of the new world, which is an unfulfilled dream that I hope will always remain unfulfilled because the moment it's fulfilled it won't be the new world anymore. It won't be a dream.

In talking about this dream and about this reality, I must mention something else. Although nobody has mentioned it today, I think it's very important. This week we are all commemorating the thirty-fifth anniversary of the death of Che Guevara. I don't know if you all knew that. He was the real dreamer, and the real guy who brought together dream and reality, in coming back to the sixties discourse, who gave us all at least an important point of departure for our work.

But I do think that Latin America in the thirties and the forties, right between the two Worlds Wars, even through the war and right after the Second World War, was a great option in a very fertile soil on which to build the new world. And that's why I think that some of the very best, freshest, and strongest modern architecture is in what we call now Latin America. I have only seen the strength of these proposals maybe in two places, one in Israel, and Frampton won't let me lie about that, as he has studied it thoroughly. Israel's modern architecture had to do with a real social dream, and that social dream also set up the basis for a fabulous architecture that met the strength and power of those modern architects. The other place was Latin America. And Latin America had the spirit and the climate and the conditions that allowed us to build, or allowed them, our predecessors, to start building that new world of modern architecture. I believe that's where the tradition of our architecture as Latin Americans really started. It was really about understanding the universal conditions of modernism and how the local tonalities reinforced or fed or informed the conditions of that universalism. It was those bases that really set up a fabulous platform to which we now march in order to understand the conditions of our generation. I strongly believe that my generation has a very important responsibility. It's the responsibility both to be universal, to be part of a global discourse, and I am sitting here at this table with at least three of the most important Latin American contemporary architects, and I'm very honored to do so. And at the same time, as these people are contributing to the global discourse by being Latin American, they are recognizing the special and unique condition, the specificities of all of these places where they are doing their work, and that work is essentially all over the world. The frontiers of Latin America, as the frontiers of anywhere else, do not exist anymore. At least they do not exist in the discourse of intellect and the discourse of the arts. And I think that is very important. I cannot believe that modernity, which is based on universality and on this global discourse, can be Mexicanized, or Venezuelanized, or Colombianized, or New Yorkized, as was mentioned today. I think it is about the strength of this modern discourse, this universal discourse, with the tonalities of our upbringing, with the decanting of our experiences, with the knowledge of the strength and the power of the places where each of us has the opportunity to build our own world. Thank you very much. [APPLAUSE]

Mario Gandelsonas

I would like to open the discussion first to ourselves—I'm going to be selfish—and I promise that, at a certain point, we are going to open the discussion to the audience. So is anyone interested in responding or in adding comments? I've seen you writing some notes. [LAUGHTER]

Rafael Viñoly

I do have a general comment. It seems to me that what Enrique so clearly spelled out is the possibility of not being labeled in a way that is actually counteracted by an insistence on revision of the past. It seems to me that there is a geographic condition, there is a cultural condition of identity that is at play. And as critical as it is—the pressure for universality and globalization—the truth is that there is also something about this generation of talent which I think is very special. I mean the newness and the amazing lack of past, in a way, which some of us have, is rather liberating. But it is also important to try to see that the conflict with our past, the conflict that Ruth [Verde Zein] mentioned before and to a certain extent that we all live with, is inevitably connected to a political and social condition that is really not to be dismissed. There is no way you can interpret any of this—Di Tella in the sixties, Villanueva himself or

Niemeyer himself—without understanding the political conditions in which all of that operated. Political conditions that were, to say the least, absolutely retrograde; in my view, they played out as a mechanism of repression, against which this movement has that particular value for me, regardless of its stylistic affiliation. There was a rebellion against something that wasn't just a lack of structure but a structure that operated against the constitution of this nation. . . . Bolívar actually had it right in the beginning, I think. It is precisely by understanding the similarities, and the similarities in the latter part of the twentieth century are completely connected to repression, completely connected to the inability to integrate all of those countries in the democratic system.

One more point, the IMF reference that Mario [Gandelsonas] made earlier: if you depersonalize the problem, I think that you may be really just thinking that there is only a sort of genetic, or magic, inevitable force that conditions all of this. . . .

Mario Gandelsonas

I would like to add a few more ingredients to this, very briefly. Somehow I'm going to synthesize some of the things that have been said, but I'm not going to do it with my words but rather quoting someone else. First, Ariel Dorfman, a Chilean writer born in Buenos Aires but actually raised here, in America. He came to Princeton this week and gave one of our university lectures. He lectured on civilization and barbarity, and on Latin America in the twentieth century. What Enrique [Norten] proposed immediately reminded me of Dorfman's words, so I want to bring them here. He talked about the inevitability of globalization, but he also said that for the so-called Latin American countries, it's imperative to think of an alternative to globalization, that is, a globalization that starts in Latin America and that it doesn't come from the center. [There was] a second issue he brought up. Looking into the past, into the twentieth century, he would obviously tell us there wouldn't be a possibility of nostalgia. He would find in America a longing for utopia, and it would be destined to frustration in the twentieth century—that's obvious. No one here is looking forward, as the destiny of Latin America. Finally, I wanted to quote the late Argentinian historian Marina Waisman. In reading three more books that I read after *Brazil Builds* and the Hitchcock book, I found a paragraph I felt was also very [relevant], and I wrote it just in case, and I felt that it could be very appropriate for this discussion. She proposes an architecture of divergence, instead of an architecture of resistance; we heard *resistance* here many, many times. And she speaks of an architecture that differs from the one practiced in developed countries, and she says, "To resist would mean to defend one's own territory against the assault of the outer world. To diverge is to depart from one's familiar territory in search of new courses of action, leaving aside the pressures and the chanting siren songs coming from the ruling culture." And I think that she wrote this just a few months before she died, and I'm bringing this in her memory but also I feel that it's very appropriate for this occasion. . . .

I'd also like to quote Kenneth Frampton when he said, "It's important to remember the unforgiving reality that exists beyond the reach of architecture, the colossal housing shortage in the tens of millions of units as a result of the never-ending urban growth. If it seems sometimes possible to separate architecture from the urban question in our world, in the developed world, it is certainly impossible to do that in Latin America, where the architect cannot insulate himself or herself from the appalling conditions that surround him in the Latin American metropolis." . . .

Carlos Brillembourg

I just want to add a small point, not necessarily to clarify, but to guide the discussion in a different direction. Somehow architecture is independent of the political sphere. And it is codependent on it. But of course architecture usually lasts longer than politicians. And that is an important point, because we have, in the University Central of Venezuela, another life. It is no longer the political jewel of a repressive regime, but it has now been recognized by UNESCO as a world monument.

This is something that is permanent and forms a culture. The thousands of architects who have gone through the university, and specifically the School of Architecture created by Paulina's father [Villanueva], directly identify with the architecture and with the project that was realized—although, as Paulina mentioned before, there is an existential condition in architecture which projects a society that does not yet exist, and often that society does not come into being. In this case, the society came into being in a different way than was the naive utopian idea, but perhaps in a better way. And many architects that we know have felt that they grew up in the house of learning that was built by Carlos Raul Villanueva.

Mario Gandelsonas

So I would like to open this up to the audience now. I'm sure that some of you are anxious to continue the discussion. I know it's always very difficult to start. Yes?

Audience Member

I want to ask Ruth a question. We have been talking about politics and architecture, and I wanted to put forward the example of Jaime Lerner in Curitiba. And I want to ask you what you think about these contributions as a city to our cities today? Because I come from a very polluted city in South America, and I know that this is not the only case. So I wanted to ask you what contribution do you think Jaime Lerner has made to architecture and urban planning today?

Ruth Verde Zein

Well, I am going to do something very unorthodox and discuss architecture and not politics in my answer. I'm not speaking against anyone, I'm just speaking about architecture. I think Curitiba has a lot of interesting elements, but everything under 1:500 scale is terrible. And that's very significant, for the urbanism is very good and the architecture is very bad. That's my point of view. I'm not discussing politics. Well, in a formal way, maybe. And I would like to discuss Latin America formally, also . . . the filters.

Why do we always have to discuss things through political filters? Architecture is a complex thing, as I have already said, and we must understand that from many other points of view. From the point of view of architecture, I think there are a lot of interesting things that are achieved through Curitiba, and I think they have a lot of media also, and they discovered very early that media is wonderful. If you publicize your achievements, as small as they are, they can be enlarged to a global scale.

So I'm being very critical. I'm not throwing away all those efforts from Curitiba. For example, something that I believe is better are the programs sponsored by Rio de Janeiro in the last two administrations, mainly through the hand of Luiz Paulo Conde. Those are really important, both in the urban sense and the architectural sense. So we are speaking about dwellings and housing, et cetera. We are still stopped in the sixties, but there are a lot of interesting programs and dwellings in recent years in Brazil that we do now know, we do not publicize. So Curitiba is an example, but there are many others which are not only urban achievements but aim to be good architecture and that's important, for me at least. I don't know if I answered the question.

Audience Member

Le Corbusier was used as a marker for that period. But I'm curious whether or not at that time, in the early thirties, he was really seen as a force there, really seen as an influence, or whether that came later and this is coloring our view of that period.

Lauro Cavalcanti

At that time, Le Corbusier was a sort of avant-garde writer in France. He only built weekend houses for people who were collectors of art, for instance, the brother of Gertrude Stein, Thomas Cook from the Cook. And so he saw in Latin America, and in Brazil specifically, an opportunity to build on large scale and to prove that the modern style was not only European or western European. That's one point.

But he was crucial—I can only speak of Brazil—in helping the modernists. There was a very fair trade among them and Le Corbusier. He was crucial, because he came to Brazil as an ambassador of French culture, although he was Swiss, and although he did not have space in France. Because over there, the main projects were done by the professors of the School of Fine Arts, and the projects in colonies were done by the first winners of the Rome Prize, or their first pupils. Brazil was dominated by France symbolically, but not politically. And that was made possible for Le Corbusier.

I want to make several points. One, I have praised modern architecture myself without nostalgia. I do think that studying modern architecture only interests me as a weapon for the future. I'm not interested only in the historical. But we did not mention that modern urbanism was a mess. Modern orthodox . . . it cannot even serve as something to be learned. I think that nowadays we would agree that everything that urbanists hated . . . we love. And that the nineteenth century was the best century for cities. [LAUGHTER] That's just one thing.

The other thing is, I think we should think more culturally about the meaning of local and global. I will quote the Portuguese sociologist Boaventura dos Santos. He said that in his youth—he's now in his seventies—in his youth, the Italian and French *Nouvelle Vague* movies appeared to him like the most cosmopolitan and sophisticated things, and that now he finds them parochial. And so I think that, culturally, in some way the global is the parochial with power and made global.

Kenneth Frampton

I caught Rafael's Viñoly's disease, meaning I can't stop talking! [LAUGHTER] I wanted to just make some comments. Curitiba sets me off in a way, because I agree with Ruth Verde Zein about the issue of the architecture, which is just not discussable. And I think this question of urbanism, which is that the nineteenth century was the best century for cities, but . . . in a certain sense the megalopolis is the global reality, with the exception of the historical cause that we're still able to somehow sustain with various reasons.

And what is impressive about Curitiba, of course, is public transport. And I'm sure there are other examples. In fact, I know that there is an important initiative in Bogotá, for example, equally impressive. And maybe public transport and the question of energy use and so on are terms we should really think about developing, because thinking in terms of cities in the old sense seems to be not really relevant.

But to end on this question, well, provincialism is everywhere, first of all, and something else, both positive and negative . . .

and that I address really to Rafael and to Mario, because your discourse in a way is full of understandable frustration and criticism and resentment of an experience in Argentina. But you know, the problem in some ways, I think, is that the developed world doesn't want to hear about its own underdevelopment. You know? It makes assumptions about itself, about other countries, about what you could think of as the Latin American malaise. But after all, the so-called First World is full of malaise as well.

Mario Gandelsonas

Kenneth, actually I just want to clarify . . . it's definitely not about frustration. As I said, I remember those ten years as perhaps some of my best years. So I definitely feel very frustrated with the last twenty years in terms of the political debacle in Latin America, and I suppose everyone here feels that way. Well, on the other hand, I think we could say that about a number of catastrophes around the world.

Ruth Verde Zein

I just wanted to make sure that Kenneth does not confuse the malaise of the First World with the malaise of the Third World, because they are really proportionately, geometrically different.

Max Cardillo

I've heard most of the speakers today discuss the impact of modernism on the architecture of Latin America. But modernism comes to Latin America with two shoes. One is architecture, the other is urban planning. Brasilia is perhaps the quintessential example of twentieth-century urban design. It's very utopic, it's very abstract, it's very ethereal. It's also a total failure as a city. And I'd like the speakers to discuss the impact of modern urban design and a lot of the ideas that Le Corbusier brought to Latin America in the development of urban American cities, not just in South America but everywhere.

Ruth Verde Zein

I will keep on with what Kenneth Frampton said about the megalopolis being the city of twenty-first century. And the megalopolis was begun in Brasilia. All of you know that Brasilia is just a collection of frozen images of the past from 1960 and nothing more, and so you can't say that Brasilia's a failure. It's not a failure. It's a very good city to live in, especially if you're poor. It has lots of good things, social programs, et cetera.

Brasilia is not a failure, I'm sorry to say. [LAUGHTER] In fact, Brasilia was criticized at that moment as being a city in which people took a car to go everywhere. People said that Brasilia was a collection of highways, that Brasilia had no crossing places and plazas where people could meet, that Brasilia had lots of periphery quarters where people could live. That's the description of any kind of city today anywhere in the world. So for all the critics mad about Brasilia, this is what's happened to every city. I said that in our discussion in Barcelona when we were together, Mario and I, and people said, "No, Barcelona is different." No, quite not.

The cities, the globalization, and the megalopolis have been rehearsed in Brasilia, and we do have to study Brasilia a lot and not keep on saying that it's a failure. And Brasilia is not urban planning. In fact, it's urban design more than urban planning, to be precise. I would like to live in Brasilia. It's a very nice place to live. I invite you to be there for a while.

Monica Ponce de Leon

As I see the responses, I think we're falling again into the trap of stereotyping Latin Americans as if everything is the same, and assuming that all Latin American cities have the same kinds of problems. In the case of Caracas, it's not possible. I would not blame Le Corbusier or the modern movement for our urban problems. The kind of organization that happened in Caracas after the fifties follows an American suburban model that just did not work, given our topography and given our cultural context. So the kind of traffic jams that we have, the kind of urban density that we have—this is not the result of the process of the modern movement. It's a result of following a certain line of development that just did not work in that context.

Diane Lewis

Well, I want to point out something that Paulina said in her opening comment about the relationship between form and content. And that was the point that was brought up, which I thought is an undercurrent that Enrique has emphasized in terms of a generational issue that I think is coming forth at this moment as well. And I think it's also evidenced in the optimistic approach that Carlos is making and the argument that Ruth is making as well, which does have to do with a deeper idea about the relationship of form and content in an existential sense in the modern movement. When Ruth says, "Can I please answer that question in terms of form in architecture," as if she wasn't allowed to discuss her critical understanding of the quality of a particular project architecturally—as if we could not talk that way. Or Enrique keeps talking about this generational issue. Now, as an architect, what I think is interesting is that the promise for someone like me, a postwar New Yorker from Latin America, is that it is the place of the cities of the free plan.

And so when you talk about the promise—you know, I think Joseph Rykwert is here somewhere, but when I was in London giving a lecture in 1978 Joseph Rykwert got up with a piece of chalk and did a fifteen-minute lecture on the issues of the free plan as an urban space and the political, social, and formal issues of that, and picked out the few places in the world where it had been experimented with. So the Other, for a New Yorker from the sixties generation, is not communism; it is Latin American cities. [LAUGHTER]

Carlos is making the point about the evolution of the program and promise of the program, and someone made that point in terms of the fusion of form and content, as though any of these things could ever be commandeered to hold anything but a truly humanitarian program in terms of the scale of the urban detail, which I think was Ruth's point.

So there's a constant in the criticism Ruth keeps bringing up, there's a constant assumption that the modern project can be commandeered for other purposes when in fact you know damn well that if you stand at the Lever House, New York is totally different, and it is actually different. Politically, socially, and otherwise.

So I think we're still victims. Our generation particularly is victim of a kind of unfair utopia: the constant use of this utopian communist program for the modern movement and the absolute abuse. . . you can't use the word *humanism* in any way, because humanism is passé, as we've learned from many of our colleagues. [LAUGHTER] And I think that Carlos has made that argument exquisitely today and organized this conference to have that as a tremendous impact. It has come forward, without it being just put into the area of pure poesis or pure design, or you know, certainly what we at Cooper Union suffer as the critique of our position on the urban. So I give that to you.

Joseph Rykwert

Since I was quoted by Diane, I thought I'd intervene. [LAUGHTER] Because I was also very, very shocked by a comment that came from over there that nobody seems to have picked up on, which is that at some point a government sent in inspectors to teach people how to use their houses. I think we are the first civilization in which people have to be taught how to live in a house. And the monstrousness of that . . . [APPLAUSE] doesn't seem to have struck people.

And that also made me reflect on another thing. I was also shocked by the fact that both Kenneth and Diana are nostalgic about the Soviet Union. How, after Solzhenitsyn and Robert Conquest, can one be nostalgic about it? It wasn't just a mistake. It was an unspeakable horror, and to invoke nostalgia for that seems to be—In a way it's tied in my mind with that comment about people being taught to use their houses. Because in fact one of the problems that we haven't talked about is that the architecture of the twenties and thirties did not acknowledge the importance of public space in relation to housing.

That's one of the terrible things, and that's one of the important things, I think, about the University of Caracas, because it was a modern architect creating a public space and using works of art to do so. And as two or three people have already remarked, it has survived the horrible political regime which created it and is therefore a much more important document than much of the housing that was built during that period.

Housing always seems to produce corruption. Whether it's in Argentina or in China, it's exactly the same. And I think one of the lessons that we've forgotten is that there was a movement for self-help housing after 1945. It was a movement that started, I think, in south Peru. It also started independently in India. I think it was very important. It lasted briefly. Governments don't like it.

The truth is, of course, that most of the people who move from the country into towns, whether it's in Latin America or elsewhere, don't live in government-sponsored housing. They live in *barrios* and *favelas*. And they do so also in Brazil. Maybe Brasilia is a great success, but the architect who showed me around kept two rock filers to defend himself at night. That sort of city, to me, is not really a success.

Mario Gandelsonas

Joseph, before you go, I have a question for you. While you were describing the situation, two images came to me. I don't know why. One is the social engineering in America in the fifties, in which our vast middle class in this country was socially engineered to learn how to live in a single-family house in the suburbs, and somehow this transformed entirely the notion of housing in this country. When we're talking about housing here, we're talking about the rest of the world and not about America. The other question is, while millions of people in South America live in the *favelas*, in the *villas miserias,* et cetera, tens of millions—thirty, perhaps forty million—live in single-family houses or rooms. So do you have something to say about that? . . . We're talking about the early twentieth century, but definitely not about the late twentieth century or the beginning of the twenty-first.

Joseph Rykwert

But of course the answer, the extension, the projection of the suburban house is the gated community. More and more suburban districts are turning into gated communities because they're no longer safe. Gated communities exist all over the world. . . . They're very popular in China, they're very popular in India. They are surveyed by television screens in little guard rooms and this is the future to which we are tending. My Brazilian friends' rottweilers are now substituted by television screens. This is the truth about the suburban model, which is spreading every-where and which is perhaps not as entirely salubrious as the advertisements in the American color magazines taught us in the fifties and sixties.

Mario Gandelsonas

Thanks. Terry?

Terence Riley

Actually, we're using our real estate, so we have to wind up. [LAUGHTER] One final personal story that might leave it on a different note. Due to the miracles of modern travel, I had the experience one day of spending the morning in Cancun, Mexico, and the afternoon in Havana, going from Singapore with Taco Bells to East Berlin with palm trees. And my feeling, as I went from this grotesque consumption, consuming society on one hand to a kind of throwback to a totalitarian state was: are these the only two choices? And I think that we have to agree that they're not and that's the business of the rest of the century. So thank you very much.

Mario Gandelsonas

Thank you, Terry. [APPLAUSE]

Notes

1. Architect Jaime Lerner served three terms as mayor of Curitiba, in Brazil, starting in 1971. He implemented a mass transportation system that was hailed for its efficiency and low cost.

Photo Credits

Vera Adami/Paço Imperial (courtesy of): 53 top right and bottom left, 54 bottom, 57 (all)

Fernando Albuquerque: 54 top

José Antonio Aldrete-Haas: 103 bottom, 104 top and middle, 113 bottom

Bjorg: 136

Alfred Bradler: 60

Paulo Gasparini/Villanueva Foundation: front cover, 5, 6, 8, 64 (all), 67 bottom, 72

G. E. Kidder-Smith: 39 bottom

Alejandro Leveratto: back flap, 9, 93 (all)

Jorge Francisco Liernur: 82 middle left, 85 (all), 88

F. S. Lincoln: 39 top, 45 middle

Cristiano Mascaro: front flap, 1, 2 (both), 3, 4 (both), 50, 53 top left and bottom right, back cover

Niemeyer Foundation: 42 top, 46 bottom

Armando Salas Portugal/ Barragán Foundation: 11, 100, 103 top, 104 bottom, 110 (all), 113 top

Roberto Segre: 14, 15, 16, 42 bottom, 116, 120, 125 (all), 126 (all), 129 middle and bottom, 130 (all), 133 (all)

Alfredo Testoni: 78 top

Cecilia de Torres (courtesy of): 10

Eduardo Luis Rodriguez: 129 top

Villanueva Foundation: 7, 42 top

Claudio Williams (courtesy of): 90

Kim Zwarts: 12, 13, 103 middle left, 109 (all)